Before we begin unpacking H, chance to hear from some of the people who molded and shaped the way that we think and how we live our lives. Their willingness to love us big and cheer enthusiastically in these next few pages means so much, and is a testament to the faithfulness of God in shaping each of us through community.

Sincerely,
Phillip and Destiny Deas

House Habits doesn't just tell you what to do to build a mission and stay on mission; it also gives clear and concrete handles that anyone can apply immediately to their situation. Whether you are a pastor, leader, or just starting your journey to find meaning in life, this book will help guide you along the way.

> —Scott Wilson, *Founder and CEO of RSG leaders and 415, Author,* Identity: The Search that Leads to Significance *and* True Success

One of the greatest gifts we can give ourselves, our churches, and our businesses is clarity. Clarity, or as the scripture says in Habakkuk 2:2 in reference to vision, "making it plain," is a necessary but sometimes overlooked component that equips and empowers people and organizations to run, progress, and ultimately fulfill mission. In *House Habits*, Phillip and Destiny provide readers with profound clarity on mindsets, values, and daily practices that are helpful in closing the gap between goals and mission. These practices are catalytic in creating healthy, flourishing, transformative cultures for families, churches, and businesses.

> —Jelani Lewis, *Executive Pastor, Campus Ministries, Gateway Church*

So many of us can articulate the mission and vision of where we want to go and what we want to accomplish, but we struggle to define the daily steps that will move us closer to "mission accomplished." Phillip and Destiny have crafted vital habits into clear, understandable steps that, when practiced daily, will create an atmosphere and culture that lead dreams to become reality.

—Dr. Scott Holmes, *Louisiana Assemblies of God, Superintendent, Author,* The Joseph Journey: An Unlikely Path to Greatness

Little did I know when I walked into Northpoint Community Church in 2015 that what I would learn over the next twelve months, The House Habits, would transform and shape my life, my family, and my business.

My family and I live on the other side of town; but from day one, we loved the lessons we were being taught each week by Phillip and Destiny at NCC. I noticed a unified couple who were very protective of each other. They had a selfless mentality that consistently honored one another and those who'd gone before them. As a family, Lindsi and I decided to lean in 100% to their community—the growth of ourselves, our family, and our businesses became very intentional.

It's now 2022, and I look back at how embracing these habits and being disciplined about them have laid a firm foundation for me. If I'm being completely honest, the house habits have taught me to be a better leader and I'm so excited for Phillip and Destiny to so generously give them away in a book.

The enthusiasm in their words makes me feel as if they are my biggest cheerleaders, and it keeps my focus on the mission before me, giving me the power to stay on it. Thank you, Phillip and Destiny, for your love and leadership.

—Dany Martin, *Husband, Father, Financial Advisor, Entrepreneur*

A lot of us are looking for new ways to elevate our level of success, whether it is in our personal or professional lives. Look no further, because Phillip and Destiny reveal through their own personal stories—and a lifetime of establishing their own habits—just how the things we do each day shape our days and, ultimately, affect our lives for good or bad.

I believe as you adopt these House Habits in your life, you will not only see long-term improvements but also an overall improvement in your quality of your life.

—PASTOR SHEILA CRAFT, *Co-founding Pastor, Elevate Life Church, Frisco, TX, Author,* Live Your Legacy: Live the Legacy You Want to Leave

I can't communicate to you how critical the formation of good habits is—and how difficult it is at the beginning. Thanks for communicating to the world the need to develop good habits with the assurance that if we stick to them with the end in mind, we can achieve our desired goals.

—STEVEN CABRERA , *Lt. Col. United States Air Force*

Phillip and Destiny Deas empower individuals and families to create lasting legacy in their book, *House Habits.* Their ability to communicate the "what and how" of living on mission is truly transformational. Our marriage and home have been influenced by their example for years and we know that this book will establish strength in your journey for years to come!

—DAWNCHERE AND RICH WILKERSON JR., *Founding Pastors, Vous Church, Miami*

I (Ron) met Phil and Destiny while they were students. . . . Phillip a quarterback at University of North Carolina and Destiny excelling at Duke School of Law. It only took a minute to recognize they were both champions and headed for greatness. Since then, we have had many times together as they faithfully serve on one of our global mission boards. House Habits is like getting an up-close recipe of their extraordinary lives. Every page speaks volumes about the practical ingredients that bring meaning and reward.

—Ron Lewis, *Pastor and Apostolic Leader, and Lynette Lewis, TedX speaker and corporate consultant*

HOUSE
HABITS

LIVING ON MISSION
ONE HABIT AT A TIME

PHILLIP & DESTINY DEAS

ARROWS & STONES

Cover design by: Sara Young
Cover photo by: HM Photography & Boutique

ISBN: 978-1-957369-94-5   1 2 3 4 5 6 7 8 9 10

Printed in the United States of America

This book and the House Habits are dedicated to the people of Northpoint Community Church, past, present, and future. These habits came from our house, but you have made them yours. You have taken them into your schools and businesses and squadrons. And you are the reason that Christ-centered, culture-changing community is being created every day. We love you.

CONTENTS

Foreword xi

INTRODUCTION 13

MISSION FOCUSED 15

HABITS CENTERED 35

HABIT 1 **WE LIVE ON** 45

HABIT 2 **WE LOVE BIG** 69

HABIT 3 **WE PROTECT UNITY** 83

HABIT 4 **WE HONOR CONSISTENTLY** 93

HABIT 5 **WE LEAN IN** 105

HABIT 6 **WE GROW INTENTIONALLY** 127

HABIT 7 **WE PRACTICE HONESTY** 145

HABIT 8 **WE EMBRACE DISCIPLINE** 159

HABIT 9 **WE LEAD OUT** 173

HABIT 10 **WE GIVE GENEROUSLY** 187

HABIT 11 **WE CHEER ENTHUSIASTICALLY** 197

HABIT 12 **WE STAY ON MISSION** 211

CONCLUSION 227

Endnotes 229

Acknowledgments 233

FOREWORD

Phillip and Destiny Deas have spent their lives together capturing life skills that really work. If you are a seeker and hungry for truth that can be converted in real-time into actionable steps to build a mission-focused life, *House Habits* is for you. If you have the capacity to turn introspection into an adventure and you believe that incremental change beats futility every time, you will love this book. If you are really serious about being better at the roles you fill as a son or daughter, spouse or parent, friend, worshipper, believer, or learner, you will find soulmates in this duo. This book will become a valuable reference and manual for life in so many ways.

Phillip and Destiny are extraordinary writers and communicators on any level. They passionately and energetically put into practice what they teach. Destiny is a lawyer, and as you will see in this book, she unpacks each case for change in detail and supports every suggested solution with encouraging and irrefutable evidence of personal trial and error.

Phillip, on the other hand, is a championship football coach who has turned his attention to helping individuals and corporations live as everyday champions. For Phillip, every truth is common sense and always on the lower shelves, in reach for everyone. He sees change as a challenge to master but something every logical, thinking person should passionately desire. Perhaps it is this combination of perspectives that gives Phillip the rare gift of making often-challenging principles simple and doable.

House Habits is one of those rare reads that makes you ask why it took somebody so long to write it. It is a beautifully written, witty, and honest look at how much better life can be if we are intentional about managing its common challenges.

—Pastor Denny Duron
Author, Speaker, Coach, and Pastor
Shreveport Community Church

INTRODUCTION

One of the proudest moments I've ever experienced as a leader was watching one of our church members talk on a podcast about the difference House Habits has made in his business. We never created the House Habits for a church setting. We created them out of our own home in hopes that businesses, schools, communities, and other families would benefit from the strength and stability that shared habits based on shared values based on shared mission inevitably bring. Since we started teaching the habits, we have had the privilege to watch this hope become a reality. A school system in nearby Texas implemented its own version of the House Habits, as have multiple other faith communities and businesses.

And yes, these House Habits are also the foundation of our own faith community.

I will never forget our first Sunday as lead pastors of Northpoint Community Church (NCC) in a semi-rural Louisiana town called Bossier City. We were standing in a building with three different kinds of carpet on the floor (leftover "gifts" from a local casino remodel), shiny brass ceilings, and dusty greenery in the tall skylight-type windows. The music was terrible. The sound was worse. And we were so proud.

We started with 230 people each weekend in 2013 and have seen our community grow to over 1,000. That's not the miracle. The miracle is that we still like coming to church. We want to be there. We love our community. And we trust our community to help raise our kids as we help raise theirs. We are truly in this together, and we have been able to maintain this culture of inclusion, love, and faith even as we have grown, largely because of the principles we will share in the next few pages.

This book came from our hearts to see every church, every home, every business transformed by the power of implementing mission-driven habits. So I encourage you not just to read it as our story but to consider how House Habits could impact your life, your family, and your organization.

If you happen to be in our community today, lean into this book, grow intentionally, and remind yourself that, above all, we stay on mission.

Note about perspective from Phillip: This book was a joint effort. Destiny and I built this community and this content together. However, for clarity and ease of reading, unless otherwise noted, the perspective will be my own.

MISSION FOCUSED

A mission statement is not something you write overnight ... But fundamentally, your mission statement becomes your constitution, the solid expression of your vision and values. It becomes the criterion by which you measure everything else in your life.
—STEPHEN COVEY

The Great Commission is too big for anyone to accomplish alone and too important not to try to do together.
—STEVE MOORE

Having a mission statement is not a new idea. From Stephen Covey[1] to John Maxwell[2] to the new groovy millennial life coaches, almost everyone agrees goals are easier to achieve and life becomes more intentional when you have a clear, written mission statement. That said, most of us still do not follow their sage advice. I find in my interactions that Christians are even less likely than their secular counterparts to embrace the idea of personal mission. Of course, this is a purely personal perspective, but I'm not so sure it's off. After all, we are part of the biggest mission force on planet Earth. We are Christ's hands and feet! Why define what took sixty-six books (the Bible) to reveal? I would counter that if our mission is so important, which it is, then we most certainly should be able to clearly define it, and personalize it, for anyone who asks.

//

CHRISTIAN OR NOT, EVERYONE NEEDS A MISSION.

\\\

When we transitioned into leadership at Northpoint Community Church in Bossier City, we knew our community needed an easily defined mission. Going through the process of identifying, verbalizing, and institutionalizing our mission has proven every bit as beneficial as promised. Ask anyone who has been part of our community for more than a few weeks what our mission is, and they can say it without hesitation. Ask our kids, and they can say it too. We are on the same page, speaking the same language, going after the same thing, and we are better for it.

At Northpoint, our mission is simple: "Creating Christ-centered, culture-changing community." It's an alliteration because we are, after all, church kids. It's pithy because we knew we wanted everyone to memorize it word for word. And it's our way of rephrasing the core mission of the gospel because the gospel is the only thing on Earth worth living and giving our lives for.

As we have traveled and shared with other communities, we have found that this way of phrasing the Christian mission connects far beyond our small rural community. We all have a personal mission, but we all are also responsible for this one.

Jesus, twice in the scriptures, tells us to go into all the world and make disciples. In our minds, discipleship, preaching the gospel, and baptizing people look like creating a Christ-centered, culture-changing community. After all, we aren't creating our own disciples; we are creating Christ-centered disciples. And a Christ-centered disciple of Jesus won't be a culture-acceptor. No! He will be a culture-changer. And disciples don't live alone. Instead, they live in community. Thus, our mission translates the mission of the gospel into simple components that are easy for each of us to grasp and understand. Of course, it might be simple, but it most certainly will not be easy.

CREATING

//

CREATIVITY IS THE CORE OF WHO GOD IS AND THEREFORE AT THE CORE OF WHO WE, AS IMAGE BEARERS, ARE MEANT TO BE.

\\

Creating is an active word. It requires work. Creatives are often given a bad rap in our society and in the church. We think of guys and girls in ripped skinny jeans, drinking fair trade lattes, and obsessing over fonts and aesthetics. And yet, God is described at the beginning of time as Creator. Creativity is the core of who God is and therefore at the core of who we, as image bearers, are meant to be. The book, *Called to Create*, lays out the case perfectly for who God has called each of us to be, creators of good things here on this earth.[3]

Creating, within the context of our mission, will most certainly require all the hard work and mental energy the word suggests. One does not truly create by accident. There is an intentionality at work in the process, even if there is a bit of providence in the outcome (Proverbs 16:9). We work hard to create, intentionally placing our time and energy toward the goal and trusting that God will do what only He can do in the meantime.

The Bible often uses farming metaphors, which makes sense given its original audience and the centrality that farming has to our existence. Kroger, despite personal experience, is not really where food comes from. One of my favorite verses says whatever a person sows, they will also reap (Galatians 6:7). This is often used for financial sermons, but it is much broader than that limited subject matter. The Bible is making a guarantee of divine cooperation in our creativity. After all, there is nothing that the farmer can do to make the seed grow. The farmer can put the seed inside the correct soil, feed it the correct nutrients, ensure adequate water, but there is a process that happens inside of the seed that is still yet beyond the farmer. The farmer must trust that her intentionality will be met by the cooperation of the laws and forces of nature at work within the seed. The seed must respond for all of the intentionality to have meaning.

Likewise, we admit from the outset of our mission that we are at the mercy of the God factor. We sow, we create, we spend our time and energy intentionally, but our efforts ultimately rely on the God who brings all things to life. Only He can cause the seeds we sow to blossom into the harvest we most deeply desire.

> CREATION IS SIMPLY THE ACT OF MANIPULATING WHAT IS AROUND US IN AN INTENTIONAL MANNER FOR A DESIRED OUTCOME. INTENTIONALITY IS KEY.

As we rely on God, we must choose to continue to create. Creation is simply the act of manipulating what is around us in an intentional manner for a desired outcome. Intentionality is key. One doesn't create by accident. Of course, in your mind at this moment might be the variety of unintentional discoveries of mankind that have vastly shaped our current history. Perhaps the accidental discovery of penicillin sprang to mind, or even something trivial such as Silly Putty. Yes, these were not the sought-after results, but they were the byproducts of intentional cultivation. We serve a God that does "exceedingly, abundantly above" anything that we could ask or imagine (Ephesians 3:20). This is the promise of the scriptures. And as we create, we should not hold our own results so tightly that we miss the unexpected moments of exceedingly, abundantly above that God most certainly has in store.

CHRIST-CENTERED

The spirit of Christ is the spirit of missions. The nearer we get to Him, the more intensely missionary we become.
—HENRY MARTYN

So, what are we creating? First, we are creating a community, a life, a mindset, a worldview that is Christ-centered. The scriptures tell us that Jesus is the foundation stone (Isaiah 28:16). He is not just the starting point of our lives; He must always remain the center. What we seek to create will always be Christ-centered. Judah Smith, pastor of Churchome, often says there is no need to move on from Jesus to deeper things because it doesn't get any deeper than Jesus. And that is the core of this mission statement. What we seek to create will not be dogma-centered, or theology-centered, or sect-centered, or method-centered. Instead, we will seek to place the living God at the core of all we do.

How does one create Christ-centered? It begins by looking within: Am I Christ-centered? This is a question we pose to our staff and to ourselves on a regular basis. After all, if I am not Christ-centered, then how can I create something that is? We assess our Christ-centeredness in many ways, but here are a few that might be helpful.

Is Christ the center of your time? Now, I'm not talking about quantity, necessarily. I'm talking about what gives way when there is a lack of time. Is your relationship with God, your devotional life, and Bible reading the first thing to be dropped in the crunch times? Is church attendance secondary to everything else, from sports to homework to housework? Our time is the one asset we have that does not renew and cannot be saved. We spend it as it is given to us, moment by moment. And yet, we have the capability to plan how we will spend any time we are fortunate enough to be given in the future.

IF CHRIST IS NOT THE CENTER OF YOUR DAY PLANNER, THEN HE IS LIKELY NOT THE CORE OF YOUR LIFE.

What you do with your time is the core of intentional living. And if Christ is not the center of your day planner, then He is likely not the core of your life.

The first church showed us a pattern of what it looks like to be Christ-centered. Acts 2:42 (NIV) tells us, "They devoted themselves to the apostles' teaching and to fellowship, to the breaking of bread and to prayer." The apostles' teaching correlates to the study of God's words as written in the Bible. Then we see two different community moments: fellowship and breaking of bread, which can mean holy communion. Finally, the first church valued prayer. These are the same things that we can value and place a priority on in our lives.

Maybe you are wondering how it would even be possible to make Christ the center of one's time when there seems not to be enough time to eat, never mind time to worship. We understand. We have five young children, businesses to run, a church to lead, and a marriage to pursue. Life is busy even if we only focus on the essentials. Our busy lives shouldn't be an excuse to push Christ to the side but rather an invitation to intentionally place Him at the center. After all, if I believe as a Christ-follower that my strength to parent, lead, love, work, and even problem solve comes from Him, focusing on Him as the center of my life makes sense for the benefit of all of my life.

Here are a few ideas for how you can make Christ the center of your time:

1) **Plan a time to read your Bible and pray daily.** Maybe it is the first 15 minutes when you get up. Maybe you can set aside part of your lunch break and listen to a sermon on your earbuds at your desk. Schedule the time like any appointment and do your best to keep it.

2) **Prioritize the pre-planned moments.** Church attendance is a simple way to put Christ at the center of your schedule and take advantage of a prepared environment and message. Additionally, church helps you to build friendships and community along the way.

3) **Don't get discouraged.** Learning to bring worship into your daily and weekly schedule is a challenge for everyone! You may have two days where you keep your appointment and then skip

four. Don't let that stop you from trying again. This isn't a test; it's a choice to keep putting Christ at the center of your time every day.

Is Christ the center of your conversation? Now we all know the annoying religious people who name-drop God like you would a celebrity acquaintance. And we know those who seem compelled to bring up the Bible in every conversation, often as a trump card, but sometimes just in an awkward attempt to show that they are, in fact, spiritual. That isn't what I'm talking about at all. No. Instead, I'm talking about the natural flow of conversation that comes from our hearts, not our heads. When we are in love, we can't help but mention our loved one. When we are obsessed with a new idea, it worms its way into even tangential conversations. What does our conversation show us about our love and obsession for Christ and His work on the earth?

CHRISTIANITY IS NOT JUST A PART OF OUR LIFE; IT IS THE CENTER OF OUR LIVES.

Our conversations reveal our focus. Christianity is not just a part of our life; it is the center of our lives. Therefore it shapes every aspect of our lives, from how we react to people to how we react to public policy. Now, Christians will disagree. Even the early Church disagreed on many, many things. It is how we disagree that matters. Our conversations should not be filled with vain arguments or angry and bitter words. Instead, we should remember that every person we speak of and to is a creation of our God and infinitely valuable to Him. When our conversation is full of gossip and slander, even about politicians and celebrities, we know it isn't focused on God. Bringing Christ back into the center of your conversation requires us to remember that He loved humanity, every human, so much that He died for them. That thought alone should alter the way we speak to others and even what we choose to speak about.

Is Christ the center of your decision-making process? Now I know people who have taken this concept to an unhealthy extreme. They are unwilling to make any decisions without a sign from heaven, whatever that might be. Others are unwilling to do *anything* for fear of doing the *wrong thing*. That is nonsense and completely antithetical to the gospel of grace. God has called us to do good works, and He is more than capable of redirecting our efforts if we get carried away doing the good that finds us.

What I'm talking about is whether Christ is core to our process of decision-making. Is prayer a last resort or a first response? Is the Bible a living document that informs our hearts or a dead document that dictates cold responses? Do we even know the Jesus of the scriptures well enough to ask what He would do in a particular situation?[4]

Here are a few questions to ask when you are making a decision that will help you keep Christ at the center of your process:

1) How does this choice align with my values?

2) How can I love the people in this situation as Christ has loved me?

3) What is the role God has given me in this situation? (If you are parent, boss, employee, your responsibility and your decision may change.)

4) Am I acting out of selfish ambition, anger, or some other self-centered emotion, or am I choosing to allow the fruit of the Spirit to be evident in my life?

5) Is there a clear right or wrong here? If not, what are the wise voices in my life saying?

6) Have I spent time praying and asking God to make the way forward clear?

7) Do I trust God to guide me even when I am unsure?

WE ARE FAR FROM WHERE WE WANT TO BE,
BUT WE ARE CLOSER THAN WE USED TO BE.

Creating Christ-centered in our own lives is a process that will take a lifetime. And we shouldn't be frustrated or impatient along the way. Yes, we are far from where we want to be, but we are closer than we used to be. Yes, we can find ourselves centering thoughts, conversations, decisions exclusively on ourselves, but it takes only a moment to redirect to what is important. Let's remember the words of Paul in encouragement to the early church. "And I am certain that God, who began the good work within you, will continue his work until it is finally finished on the day when Christ Jesus returns" (Philippians 1:6 NLT).

Christ-centered starts with us, but it doesn't end with us. As we seek to create Christ-centered, we must ask, "What does Jesus care about?" The Bible makes it very clear. Jesus said that He came to (1) proclaim good news to the poor; (2) proclaim freedom for the prisoners and recovery of sight for the blind; (3) set the oppressed free; and (4) proclaim the year of the Lord's favor (Matthew 25). Later on, Jesus says those who really follow Him will feed the hungry, give water to the thirsty, welcome the stranger, clothe the naked, care for the sick, and visit prisoners (Matthew 25). Jesus speaks often about the poor and meeting the real needs of those around us.

IF JESUS CARES ABOUT THE REAL NEEDS OF THOSE AROUND US, THEN WE MUST CARE TOO.

If Jesus cares about the real needs of those around us, then we must care too. And more than care, we must act. Creating Christ-centered means that we build our lives and institutions around what Jesus cared about most: people. And not just the people who are easy to be around because they don't really need us, but rather people who are in need. Need doesn't always look like someone who is hungry or needs money or material things. Often those most in need want what is most precious to us: our time. The lonely senior, the overwhelmed first-time parent, the grieving widower, the frightened young adult, all need deeply. They don't need another sermon or cookie or pat on the head. They need real time, real communication, real wisdom, real vulnerability, a real you. One of the great deceptions of Christianity is when people become a distraction from our mission rather than the core of our mission. Somehow we can be deceived to think that Christianity is more about the rules we follow and the deeds we do than the people around us we are called to love and serve.

Jesus loved people. He took time not just to meet their needs and heal them but to talk to people and get to know them intimately. As Christ-followers, we must go even further and serve others with a humility that has at its core the old Quaker saying, "but for the grace of God there go I."[5] In truth, the Church is just a community of broken people who Jesus is using to love other broken people. There is no reason to hide our brokenness in humiliation or despair. Instead, we should be honest, confess, share, and help each other along the journey. And it is amazing that the more we share and are honest about our own struggles, the more people look beyond us to see Christ.

IT IS EASIER TO RAGE AGAINST ISSUES THAN TO CARE FOR PEOPLE.

When we are Christ-centered, we put people in front of issues. It is easier to rage against issues than to care for people. It is easier to make grand Twitter statements than to love and listen and rely on the Holy Spirit to do for others what He has graciously done for us. When we commit to creating Christ-centered, we are committing to building something that Jesus would be proud of, not something that makes us feel better or superior.

CULTURE-CHANGING

In some ways, if we truly grasp what it is to be Christ-centered, culture-changing will be redundant. However, for clarity, it is helpful for us to be reminded that we are NOT culture-acceptors; we are culture-changers. Human beings have a tendency to blend. When our oldest daughter started school, she started at mid-term in first grade. Coming from a home environment where she had a lot of freedom to explore and learn on her own, I was a bit concerned she would not do very well sitting in a regular classroom. Her teacher, however, was never worried. The teacher explained to me that she had created an intentional culture in her classroom of respect and obedience, and any new child would feel the cultural pressure to blend. And she was right. My daughter never had a problem in the transition. The culture taught her everything she needed to know. She accepted the culture. She blended.

Blending is good in many ways, especially if you are five and starting school, but as Christ-followers, blending with the world can be deadly to our mission. Our mission isn't to fit in. Rather, it is to be personally transformed and allow that personal transformation to impact the world around us. We shouldn't adopt the culture around us if it leads us away from the example of Jesus. The apostle Paul warns us, "Don't copy the behavior and customs of this world, but let God transform you into a new person by changing the way you think. Then you will learn to know God's will for you, which is good and pleasing and perfect" (Romans 12:2 NLT). The New International Version says, "Do not conform . . ." In other words, do not blend in with this world. We are called to be culture-changers.

It is easier to change culture when we have our own culture. One of the things we teach our children is what we call "the Deas way." Not everyone does things the way we do as a family, and that is okay. However, we expect our children to carry our culture with them into every situation. If they are with kids who are disrespectful or mean or say unkind things, we expect them to push back and conform not to those children but to "the Deas way." As Christians, we have something more powerful than a family culture; we have a Holy Spirit-inspired kingdom culture that is carried with us and empowered from the inside out.

I DON'T TRY TO FIT IN WHERE I DON'T BELONG. I WILL SEEK TO CONNECT, BUT I WON'T CONFORM.

The beginning of culture-changing is really understanding we do not belong. I don't try to fit in where I don't belong. I will seek to connect, but I won't conform. We were created for heaven. And when we keep heaven in mind, it motivates us to be culture-creators, culture-changers here on earth. C. S. Lewis said, "If you read history you will find that the Christians who did most for the present world were precisely those who thought most of the next. It is since Christians have largely ceased to think of the other world that they have become so ineffective in this." So, daydream about heaven. Remind yourself you are not of this world, your culture is not dictated by its preferences, and you are not meant to belong.

When we understand that we are culture-changers, not culture-acceptors, then we begin to look for things within our culture that must change. At NCC, we focus on the cultural issues within our hearts and in our house first. We don't rage against outsiders or those who disagree with us, but rather we ask God to change us first. And believe me, there is enough to keep God very busy. We see culture change as a whirlpool; its power comes from its ever-widening centrifugal force. Seeing culture change as emanating from the inside out necessarily means the highest intensity, highest pressure to change, is at the center. As the church, we must allow God to change our own culture, our way of thinking, religious preferences, and keep changing us all along the way. We have to be ground zero for culture change.

Even more personally, culture change starts with me. When we commit to create culture-change, we are committing to a lifetime of being personally challenged and shaped by the Holy Spirit. We are putting our most sacred methods and experiences on the altar and saying, "Not my will but thine" (Luke 22:42), not as a moment in time but as a lifestyle choice. We are choosing to get comfortable with being uncomfortable. And in the midst, we are choosing the greatest adventure of them all.

COMMUNITY

Culture-change alone is not sustainable. It must be created within and throughout a community. And creating community is difficult. Creating culture-changing community is more difficult still.

> WE FIND CLARITY AND CONFIDENCE AND
> TRUTH IN THE MIDST OF CONFLICT.

Community means more than one. And where there is more than one, there may be conflict. Conflict is not a bad thing. In fact, we find clarity and confidence and truth in the midst of conflict. Conflict forces us to see what we might wish to ignore and to explain what we wish was understood. And creating community means not being afraid of conflict but embracing it as part of the creation process. Culture doesn't just change because I change alone. Culture begins to change when we change together.

We must intentionally create community. Community does not simply create itself. There is a common concept that says we don't need each other, and church is an outdated institution of the past. I strongly disagree. The local church community is where Christ-centered, culture-changing comes together in strength and begins to be a force for good beyond the church walls, beyond religion, beyond programs and methods and measurable matrixes. We want to create a community to support our own personal desire to be Christ-centered, a community that won't allow us to accept culture, a community that pushes us all to be more intentional, to create space for the Holy Spirit to do the work in us He promised to do.

It isn't enough to become a Christ-centered, culture-changing person; we must create community. And creating community is hard work. We have to prioritize community in our schedules. We have to find ways to work together in peace and unity. We have to deal with all the issues that arise from doing life together. Those "have to" statements can make community creation seem so overwhelming that we want to just quit and become a church of one! It is true that it might be easier to do life and Christianity alone, but isolation is not God's plan. He wants us to live in community together as a testimony to the world of what He can do. Jesus said the world would know we were His disciples—Christ-centered culture-changers—by our love for each other (John 13:35). That looks a lot like community to me.

> COMMUNITY MEANS INTENTIONALLY OPENING UP MY LIFE TO OTHERS IN TERMS OF TIME AND ATTENTION, EVEN WHEN IT IS INCONVENIENT.

If our mission is, in part, to create community, then how does that happen? First, community means more than just me and my family. That seems obvious, but it isn't. Community means intentionally opening up my life to others in terms of time and attention, even when it is inconvenient. If you are wondering how to create community, keep reading. These House Habits are part of our answer to that age-old question.

MISSION ISN'T ENOUGH

A mission is great, but how does mission translate into daily life? We found people were excited about the mission but frustrated because they didn't know what to expect in the short term. A mission is not a short-term goal. This mission is not even a long-term goal. So, how do we take creating Christ-centered, culture-changing community into the every day of every life connected to our church? For us, it was the words "every day" that sparked the next steps.

The movies are made up of the one day that defined a life, but they usually show all the days spent preparing for that one moment in a three-minute montage set to a popular and very motivational song. As viewers, we get the idea that the big moments define us when in reality, success is made up of lots of little choices that incrementally move us toward that big moment or that big opportunity. You don't feel any different on your birthday because you have been gaining that milestone, that year, that marker, day by day. Your birthday simply announces to everyone that you have arrived. Likewise, the elite athlete isn't defined by the Super Bowl win; he is confirmed by it. His daily regimen results in the big moment.

DAILY IS WHAT CREATING CHRIST-CENTERED, CULTURE-CHANGING COMMUNITY LOOKS LIKE.

After all, didn't Jesus say we would need to take up our cross daily in order to follow Him (Luke 9:23)? His mission isn't one defined by big moments. Instead, it is the daily sacrifices, choices, obedience, which make us into the disciples His Word describes. Daily disciplines, daily choices, daily obedience. The person who has a great life at fifty is most often one who had great days, which turned into great weeks, great months, great years, and great decades. Yet, we often dismiss the daily as too small to focus on, too small to warrant our planning and attention. If we do not make our mission daily, we will not achieve it at all.

So the question arises, what does creating Christ-centered, culture-changing community every day look like? What would be the daily disciplines that would result in the mission moving ahead?

Within a staff, there is a tendency to assume everyone is on the same page. It is when decisions are being made that we can see whether we are creating a common intentional culture. Within our staff, conversations and decisions soon showed that while we had a clear mission, we had no clear basis for culture-driven decision-making. We weren't in sync. We all loved Jesus, were committed to the cause and were excited about church, but our decisions didn't show a common framework of cultural values outside these basic few. That left a choice: micro-manage every decision or create a common culture that would lead to better and more consistent culture-driven decision-making. Like most churches, businesses, and families, life was moving too fast for everyone to weigh in on every decision. We needed something more than just a list of do's and don'ts. I needed something to help us make more consistent decisions without succumbing to the horrors and manmade misery of robotic bureaucracy.

Mission was great, but we needed something more.

MINDSET COMES FROM MISSION

You cannot achieve your mission or any mission without the proper mindset. Long before Dr. Carol Dweck or Dr. Caroline Leaf made this idea famous,[6] the Bible said to change your life by changing the way you think (Romans 12:2). Having grown up connected to the "Think. Be. Do." culture of Keith Craft and Elevate Life Church in Frisco, Texas,[7] we knew that mindset was an important part of our personal faith journey. What we had not yet realized is that mindset would also be core to the evolution of our church culture as well.

> LEADERS CANNOT BE RAISED UP IN THE GREENHOUSES OF FAITH. THEY MUST BE GIVEN ROOM TO GROW AND EXPLORE AND LEARN.

As we began to study and teach on mindset, godly mindsets prescribed by the Bible, we realized the true power of mindset was in how it predetermined many decisions. This is also not a new idea, but it hit us like a ton of bricks falling out of the back of a pickup truck on I-10 (we are from Louisiana, so at least one pickup truck joke is obligatory). As we were growing, we could no longer be a part of every meeting, every conversation, every decision. And we had no desire to be! Raising up leaders has always been a big part of our own personal mission. And leaders cannot be raised up in the greenhouses of faith. They must be given room to grow and explore and learn. We did want the people who came into our church for help and encouragement to be dealt with in a consistent way. So, how could we give freedom to grow and still encourage consistency in decision-making? Our team needed a way to predetermine certain decisions in a variety of circumstances. And mindset provided the key.

Many people, at this point in their own personal or corporate development process, create core values. Core values are a great way to achieve a common mindset. For example, if the customer is always right, then you know as a salesperson your job is to meet the needs of the customer regardless of the inconvenience; the value predetermines your response to their need. If "an empty seat is a serious matter,"[8] like one church in Oklahoma has stated, then I have predetermined how I will react to an empty seat—I will invite someone! We love this idea!

Another route people take to help establish consistent culture-driven decision-making is to establish practices. These are a set of "if, then" statements or actions. For example, if someone walks up angry, then you will say, "I can see you are angry. How can I assist you?" If a client attacks your character, then you will call a supervisor. If your spouse comes home late, then you will give him grace. The value determines your response, but it is implemented through specified practices. Usually, practices are the way that core values find expression.

Ultimately we settled on a combination of the two, and we called this combination a House Habit. House Habits are how our culture translates the mission into the every day. They establish the cultural expectations we have of each other, ourselves, and the future. If we are unhappy with our relationships, we look to the habits that form the basis of those relationships. These habits fill in the gaps between mission and goals. Goals are the specific tasks I assign myself to complete my mission. Habits are the way I go about every goal, every task, every interaction.

As you intentionally create your own family, church, organizational culture, choose House Habits that help you make decisions in advance of conflict. As you will see, each of our habits is tailored to cause us to think a certain way, act a certain way, and react a certain way. However, none of these habits are task driven. Tasks, goals, and methods change, but if I have the right habits, I will be able to easily adapt and stay on mission.

Over the next few chapters, we will go over our chosen House Habits. Some of these may speak to you. Others may not fit your environment. I encourage you to see each chapter as an opportunity to consider how you think, what you expect, and how you react within your given cultural spheres. Are you carrying culture with you, or are you conforming to the cultures you walk into? Do not get hung up on the decision process of which House Habits will underlie your life or your organization. Instead, focus on the process of examining what is closest to your heart and what habits would most support that desired culture and help you achieve your mission.

Say It Again:

- Mission is the basis of creating or changing culture in your home, work, or church.
- Your mission determines mindset—what is important to you.
- You need more than a mission to create the culture that will see the mission through.
- Values are important; practices are key. We have combined the two into something called House Habits.
- House Habits capitalize on consistent behavior and pre-determined values to create clear expectations that help shape and create culture.

Make it Personal:

What is your mission as an individual? Church? Organization? If you don't have one, read a few books or articles and begin thinking about what is most important to you. If you have a mission, is it connected to what you do every single day? Is it specific and broad enough to move you toward a specific end or carry past the end of your life?

Take a moment to evaluate your life:

- Are you living intentionally? Creating the life you want to live?
- Are you living Christ-centered? We aren't just talking about your beliefs or personal thoughts. What about your actions? Do your allegiances show that you care about what Christ cares about?
- Are you living as a culture-changer or culture-acceptor?
- Are you living and creating community? Do you see yourself as a one-man show? Is the success or failure of your organization based on you? Are you putting yourself in the uncomfortable place that we call community?

Use your own mission statement to do the same. Does your daily life reflect the mission that you have laid out as a guiding force for your life? Do the priorities of your organization reflect the mission? What changes would you need to make to bring those things in line?

HABITS CENTERED

*Excellence is an art won by training and habituation. We do
not act rightly because we have virtue or excellence, but we
rather have those because we have acted rightly. We are what
we repeatedly do. Excellence, then, is not an act but a habit.*
—Aristotle

HABITS ARE FOUNDATIONAL

*You can't build a great building on a weak foundation. You must have
a solid foundation if you're going to have a strong superstructure.*
—Gordon B. Hinckley

O ur habits shape our days. Once, we had the chance to talk to a
highly successful consultant from Singapore. She founded her
own company, is one of the best in the world in her field, and is by every
measure a true leader. When we asked what she felt was the basis for
her incredible success, her answer was surprisingly simple. She said, "I
just try to have really good days." She understood good days turn into
good weeks and good weeks into good months, and good months into
a good life. Her success was in focusing on the daily habits that bring
about lifelong success. If our habits shape our days, then our habits
will ultimately determine the course of our lives.

HABITS FORM THE FOUNDATION
FOR EVERY CHAMPION.

This daily approach is similar to the one I've seen successful coaches use on the athletic field. I spent over a decade of my life as a football coach. I began every week by encouraging the players to have a great Monday, the hardest day to have a good practice on any level. "Good Mondays create good Tuesdays. Good Tuesdays turn into good Wednesdays, Thursdays, and ultimately to success on game days. Winning weeks lead to winning seasons. And at the end of a winning season is a championship." Days and weeks build on each other. Momentum is created, and at the core was a habit of leaning into Monday practice. Habits form the foundation for every champion.

The storms of life tend to expose our foundations. Jesus describes a storm as recorded in the gospel of Luke:

These words I speak to you are not mere additions to your life, home-owner improvements to your standard of living. They are foundation words, words to build a life on. If you work the words into your life, you are like a smart carpenter who dug deep and laid the foundation of his house on bedrock. When the river burst its banks and crashed against the house, nothing could shake it; it was built to last. But if you just use my words in Bible studies and don't work them into your life, you are like a dumb carpenter who built a house but skipped the foundation. When the swollen river came crashing in, it collapsed like a house of cards. It was a total loss. (Matthew 7:24-25; 27-28 MSG)

The interesting thing in Jesus' story is that, as casual observers, we can't tell who has a firm foundation and who doesn't. That's often the case in life as well. Nice house, painted shutters, two-car garage. They show up on Sunday at least once a month, attend a small group, maybe even give. Their kids attend good schools, achieve passable marks, and are in all the right clubs with similarly attired friends. Then, a storm hits, adversity strikes, and the foundation is revealed. You can't fake it in the heat of the battle. What's in you is going to come out of you.

Maybe you have had that moment when the storm tested the foundations of all you had built. What did you find? We see in the storm whether we were working the Word of God into our lives or working our life around the words of God. And the difference between the two is all the difference in the world.

If we are going to build a strong Christ-centered, culture-changing community, then it will require a firm foundation. And that is why habits must be foundational and not just nice additions to our lives. Discipline thrives in a habit-based environment. So, discipleship will demand habits. Have you ever visited a college football practice? It is intense. Yet, there is a rhythm to every moment. There are habits to the discipline. There is consistency of form and fundamentals that reach back even to the early days of middle school football. In fact, the further into the professional sports arena you delve, the more you will find people obsessed with the fundamentals, sharpening and honing their habits. Why? Because in the middle of the big game, your foundation will be exposed, your commitment to the fundamentals will show through, and your habits will either honor you or betray you.

IF YOU DEVELOP DAILY HABITS OF SUCCESS, THEN YOU WILL MAKE DAILY SUCCESS A HABIT.

The truth is, we will never grow beyond our habits. If you develop daily habits of success, then you will make daily success a habit. Habits take work to establish, but once they are established, they begin to establish you.

GOOD HABITS ARE INTENTIONAL

Everyone has habits. When we got married, Destiny and I had completely different ways of dealing with our car keys. We both had habits. I would come into the house and put my keys down on the corner of the counter next to my wallet and watch. And every morning, I would pick them up, walk out the door, and go to work. On the other hand, Destiny would walk into the house and put the keys wherever her hands happened to place them. And not surprisingly, it took her significantly longer to leave the house in the morning because she had to allocate time to look for her keys. We both had habits that dictated what we did with our keys. However, one of us was being intentional, and it made all the difference.

You will live either by design or default. When we allow our habits to be formed by default, it can result in fear, worry, negativity, cynicism, prejudice, and other energy-wasting emotions. Often, it is not the bad intentions but the lack of intention that causes us to miss out on the benefits of living a life by design.

Our habits keep our hearts in check and force us to flourish in new areas! Bad habits are easy to form; they conform to the culture around us and often within us. Good habits are hard to acquire and maintain; they are counter-cultural. Bad habits steal from you. Good habits give life to you. Bad habits limit you, but good habits will liberate you. Our lives, homes, churches, institutions, communities will never be stronger than our habits. And habits are reflected in our daily choices.

Eventually, we have to make a decision: live detached or live determined. When our habits evolve by default, we eventually feel detached. After all, it appears as though our lives are moving past us without much action on our part. We are victims, not agents in our story. Living by design, on the other hand, requires us to be determined, to fight against the cultural stream, and to live on purpose every day.

Eventually, Destiny tired of looking for her keys in the mornings and began placing them strategically next to mine on the counter. And that is where you will find them if you look today. Those first few weeks of habit change took a lot of effort, failure, and reminders. Now, she feels like she has left something undone if she does not put the keys in their appropriate place. We both notice. It is on automatic. Our keys have become safe in the midst of a habit.

HABITS ARE THE BASIS OF CREATING THE LIFE THAT GOD HAS ALREADY CREATED YOU TO LIVE.

This autopilot benefit is why we stress intentional habits. We believe as you seek to create a Christ-centered, culture-changing community where you are, habits will create the environment where you and those you love can flourish. Habits are the basis of creating the life that God has already created you to live.

HABITS ARE TRANSFORMATIONAL

GOOD HABITS SERVE YOU WHILE BAD HABITS FORCE YOU TO SERVE THEM.

Too many times, we are waiting on our character to change or our desires to change when what we need to do is change our habits which will, in turn, transform our character and desires. A habit has nothing to do with skill, talent, or gifting. In fact, that is one reason habits are often overlooked as a powerful force in our lives. Habits aren't sexy. A habit is something you must force into your life because you want the result of that habit so badly the price is worth it. We don't create habits just for habits' sake! No! We create habits for the results they offer. Destiny changed where she put her keys because she was tired of searching for what did not have to be lost! Good habits serve you while bad habits force you to serve them.

Maybe you don't like the habits you are living with. Well, old habits are hard to break. And new habits are hard to form, but it is possible. Change doesn't happen just because you have a new desire. Change happens because you are making new decisions. Many people have the right desires but do not create the habits necessary to institutionalize new daily decisions.

Let's look at some definitions for the word habit.[9]

+ Habit is defined as "an acquired behavior pattern followed until it has become almost involuntary."

- ◆ Acquire is defined as "to gain for oneself through one's actions or efforts."
- ◆ Behavior is defined as, "the way in which one acts or conducts oneself, especially toward others."
- ◆ Pattern is defined as a "model used for making things."

We must work, gain for ourselves through action or effort, the kind of behavior we want so we can create the life we want. These behaviors must be done regularly until they have become almost involuntary. In other words, we must force now so that we can flourish later. My self-discipline in every day will help my self-control in every moment. When I'm disciplined to read, pray, think, and speak gratitude, then it is easier to have self-control when dealing with an unhappy client, angry spouse, or frustrated child.

GOOD INTENTIONS DO NOT BECOME GREAT ACTIONS WITHOUT THE POWER OF HABIT.

Habit takes us from having the right attitude to having the right actions. Good intentions do not become great actions without the power of habit. Why? Because when our hearts are fickle, our habits will keep us faithful to the mission. Habits exist to help reinforce what you have already determined to be important.

HABITS WORK TOGETHER

Everything is about everything. —DENNY DURON

No habit is an island. Our habits work together to build our life. Just like a single brick lying in a field does not a wall make, so too a single habit will not be enough to build what we want in our life.

You and I may want to be healthy, but simply adding a salad at meals won't be sufficient. We will have to add other habits to live a truly healthy lifestyle. We need to build a web of habits that can support our lives and the future we see for ourselves and our communities.

That is why the next chapters are filled with twelve habits that in our house help us build the life we want to live.

These habits are divided into groups of four:

Community: We Live On, We Love Big, We Protect Unity, We Honor Consistently.

Transformation: We Lean In, We Grow Intentionally, We Practice Honesty, We Embrace Discipline.

Impact: We Lead Out, We Give Generously, We Cheer Enthusiastically, We Stay on Mission.

Together, each work to help us achieve something essential in our lives. After all, we are built to connect to God and others, grow in every area, and impact the world around us. Community leads to transformation, which increases our impact, and on and on the process grows.

As you can probably see, the habits work across the list in the same way. If you intentionally connect to God and others and choose to grow in every area to lead yourself and those around you, your impact will be bigger and better and stronger. Like a circle, this process will lead you to deeper connections, greater growth, and deeper impact.

Habits work together! In the next few chapters, we will talk about Living On, Leaning In, and Leading Out as individual habits. Together, they combine to be even more powerful! Living on (not quitting) puts you in the position to lean in, which gives you the proper posture to lead out into the gaps around you. The same goes for Loving Big, Growing Intentionally, and Giving Generously. Loving big will force you to grow intentionally, allowing you to give more generously than you could ever imagine. This goes across the board for our House Habits, but it is the same for you too!

Understanding how your habits work together is key to making habits work for you instead of against you. As you read the rest of this book, don't just think about each habit as a silo, operating all alone, but imagine them as a web of habits combining to provide a firm foundation for a life lived on mission.

THREE KEYS TO HABIT FORMATION:

1) **Decide** – The decision-making process takes a lot of emotional and mental energy. Think about a habit that you need to achieve your mission. Attacking more than one, two at the most, is not advisable. Once you have decided what habit you want to create, write it down, and put it in a prominent place. Remind yourself this habit is not up for discussion. You have already decided.

2) **Measure your progress** – We have to give attention to our intention. Habit creation is a process. There will be wins and losses along the way. Celebrate the wins and learn from the losses. Whatever you do, don't stop measuring progress, and don't stop working toward your ultimate goal of changing your habit. If it is a financial habit, set a time once a week to evaluate the data. Make sure that you can measure what you are trying to change so you can evaluate your progress. Habits are not goals. So, there shouldn't be a "goal" but rather progress toward consistency.

3) **Be accountable** – You are more likely to stick with your plan if you are accountable to someone else. Look for an accountability structure that motivates you. Is it a friend you can confide in? A spouse who will remind you? A small group? Remember, if it doesn't hurt, it won't help. So, don't be accountable to the person who will let you off the hook. Empower the people in your life to truly encourage your progress!

Say it Again:
- Habits are foundational. Our life is built by the habits we allow and intentionally cultivate.
- Good habits must be intentionally cultivated. While bad habits often occur by default, good habits usually require intentional cultivation. The good habits we get "for free" were often paid for by someone else's intention.
- Habits are transformational. If we want to change our lives, we must also make an effort to change our habits. Habits take time and effort to put into place. Once in place, they work for us and help us to stay on track.
- Habits work together. One good habit can often lead to other good habits. There is a compounding effect when good habits are stacked one on top of the other.
- Three keys to habit formation:
  › Decide
  › Measure Your Progress
  › Be Accountable!

Make it Personal:
- Think about your daily routine. Where are your habits hurting and helping you?
- How would new habits make your life easier?
- Can you think of habits that would allow you to better live out God's mission for your life?
- What habits would you like to cultivate?

Pick one and come up with a plan to work that habit intentionally into your life. Who will you tell about your new habit today? How will you measure your progress? Who will you be accountable to?

WE LIVE ON

Never, never, never give up. —WINSTON CHURCHILL

Life is filled with moments. Some of those moments are exciting, and others are exasperating. There are seasons when you can't stop smiling and others when you aren't sure you will ever be able to smile again. We can choose through it all—the good and bad, the sad and ugly—to live on and not quit. We live on is the first of twelve habits for a reason because if you don't establish this habit, then none of the others will ultimately matter.

THE CORE OF LIVING ON IS CHOOSING, IN ADVANCE, THAT QUITTING IS NOT AN OPTION.

The core of living on is choosing, in advance, that quitting is not an option. I love sports; no one loves two-a-days. Let me explain. In football, there is a tradition where practices are held twice a day in August. In Louisiana. Outside. If you know anything about Louisiana in August, you know it is hot, humid, and miserable. When I went to college, I thought I was fully prepared for the pain of the pre-season. I was wrong. My first fall with the mighty Tarheels of North Carolina was brutal. We practiced on the turf, which is so hot in the summer that you can see the heat waves coming off the ground, and I showed up to camp sick enough to be miserable but not sick enough to miss the workout. It was awful. Our strength and conditioning coach was nicknamed Mad Dog. I was convinced in three days that he had earned and possibly chosen that nickname as a warning to incoming freshmen. It was harder than I could have ever imagined. I fought through it. I hurt through it. The one thing I did not have to go through was the mental analysis of whether to quit. That decision had already been made. It was a habit. So, when things got a little hot, I had the energy to concentrate on the challenge in front of me rather than wondering whether I should even be in the game.

That habit came from a family that didn't quit. We didn't have to play sports, but if we chose to play, we were going to give our absolute best and stick it out through the entire season. After the season was over, we could reassess, but not in the midst of the commitment. If we lost, we lived on. If we won, we lived on. If we had to run sprints or recover from an injury, we lived on. If we played, we lived on. If we rode the bench, we lived on. Quitting was not an option.

Maybe you didn't grow up in that kind of family. Maybe you have watched the people closest to you quit when you needed them most. Maybe you are thinking of quitting right now. Don't! If you quit now, you won't see what is next. And the lessons from the pain of working through the problems of today are dwarfed by the harvest those lessons can bring tomorrow.

IF WE CANNOT LIVE THROUGH THE TRAGEDY OF TODAY, THEN WE WILL NEVER EXPERIENCE THE TRIUMPH OF TOMORROW.

Living on sets our focus on tomorrow. It's easy to keep replaying what happened yesterday, to deconstruct every decision and every mistake, to live life looking in the rearview mirror. We can't control or change what happened back there. We can choose to learn the lesson and leave the depression. Sometimes, we have to literally dig a grave and leave the mistake and failure and disappointment behind.

I played college football in the days of VHS tapes. Every game was filmed, and we watched that film the day after the game to learn all the lessons. Coaches were insistent that we watch film. And often, we would watch a film more than once to make sure that we saw every tendency and corrected every error. There were exceptions. For a particularly awful game or particularly disappointing game, some coaches would determine that it was time to bury the tape. There was only the one VHS. So, this was a real decision! He and maybe a few key players or coaches would go to the game graveyard, dig a hole, bury it, and walk away. Why? Because that failure was in the past, and it was time to move on.

WHAT ARE YOU CARRYING WITH YOU THAT NEEDS TO BE BURIED?

What are you carrying with you that needs to be buried? It's hard to focus on the future when your past is calling your name, living on your nightstand, and occupying your brain. Maybe you can take a page out of a very old playbook. Write down the mistake you can't get over. Write down what you've learned. Write down what you feel. Then, put it in an envelope, go into the yard, dig a hole, and bury it. Stare at that little patch of mud and determine that you will not allow what you buried to follow you when you walk away. It's time to move on to what is next.

So, how do we develop this habit of living on in our lives? We must first focus on what we are saying. Our words are so powerful! If we are constantly using negative language like "I can't," "It's impossible," "There is no way forward," "I've already screwed everything up," it is going to be very hard to keep moving forward in our lives. Our words don't have to be dishonest, but our feelings do not determine what is true. You may feel like it's hopeless. That does not mean that it is hopeless. However, if you believe it is hopeless, keep saying it is hopeless, and act like it is hopeless, you will likely live out that reality.

Our daughters say a declaration every morning. Part of the declaration states, "I listen well. I work hard. I never give up." They say this every single day. Why? Because it is natural to quit. And that is why we have to cultivate the habit of living on through our words. What is your general tone and response? What do you say when presented with a novel idea, challenge, or setback? Do you instill courage into yourself and others in the moment or steal courage through negativity?

HOPE COMES WHEN WE SPEAK LIFE INSTEAD OF DARKNESS INTO THE MOMENT.

Let's be clear: speaking positive words isn't about ignoring the issue in front of us. You may be facing and probably are facing real challenges. Speaking positive is choosing a bigger truth over our current emotions. We cannot move forward without living on, but who wants to live on without hope? Hope comes when we choose to reframe the current crisis in light of the big picture. Hope comes when we speak life instead of darkness into the moment. There is always reason to despair. Yet, there is also always reason to hope.

So, what can we focus on to help us not give up? What words can remind us that tomorrow is coming and giving up today won't prevent its dawn or make it better? What ideas can anchor us when it feels like life will capsize our boat? Here are a few handles we have found while navigating through the ups and downs of life in community.

1) YOUR MISSION

As we said in the beginning of the book, everything revolves around mission. Our mission and values guide and anchor us and are core focal points as we cultivate the habit of living on. If our mission is to create

Christ-centered, culture-changing community, we most certainly will need to not give up to see that mission accomplished. If one of our values is grit, then giving up is certainly not an option! How do we leverage mission into a mindset of not giving up? We write the mission down. We review it. We believe we can accomplish it. And we take steps every single day towards it.

When I fail at a task, I remind myself that I still have a mission to accomplish. Let's think of it this way. Imagine, prior to the interstate system and internet, you were told to go to Chicago from Los Angeles to deliver something essential. You had to hand deliver it. No other options! Someone gave you a car and a map. You jumped on Route 66 and started going. Along the way, the car breaks down. What do you do? You can't just stop! There is a mission! So, you buy a train ticket in Sante Fe. Then the train has a breakdown. Gotta keep going! You ask a kind couple at the station to give you a lift. And finally, you make it to Chicago and hand deliver your message. Would you be bummed that you didn't make it in the car by the original mapped route? No! What matters is the mission.

When I see my problem as a project rather than a pit of despair, I access the creative power necessary to move forward.

We have to choose to treat setbacks and even painful moments not as mission-ending and life-defining moments but obstacles on the path. When I see my problem as a project rather than a pit of despair, I access the creative power necessary to move forward. Living on becomes a habit because I've pre-decided that there will be trouble AND that I have the power and ability to overcome any challenge that comes my way.

So, next time you hit a snag or even blow out a tire on life's road, take a moment, process, but then use your words to remind yourself that the mission is still going. **"I'm still on a mission"** is a great reset phrase.

2) YOUR FUTURE SELF

A trick that Destiny uses when feeling particularly unmotivated to have a hard conversation or even to clean out her closet is to imagine her today efforts as a gift to her future self. It seems so simple, but focusing on your future self can help you to live on today and not quit. When deciding whether to study hard for that test or blow it off and go to the party, imagine which will help your future self the most. How will your Monday self feel if you choose to start the week with church versus sleeping in?

The next step is not just to imagine your future self but begin to talk to your future self in your weak moments. "Future Phillip, you are going to be thrilled with the energy you get from this workout." "Future Destiny, in three hours after this tough meeting, you are going to feel so much lighter. It's going to be amazing living without that hanging over your head." That may seem crazy, but it is a wonderful way of focusing yourself on the future. And when you are focused on the future, when you visualize your future-self living in that future, you are more likely to make better decisions in the now.

If you think this is just hocus pocus, listen to what researchers found when studying the effect of visualizing your future self on behavior. "Many people feel disconnected from the individuals they'll be in the future and, as a result, discount rewards that would later benefit them. But brief exposure to aged images of the self can change that behavior."[10] Just viewing an image, briefly, of your aged self can change behavior! How much more a regular focus on the future self!

When we decide to live a life that lives on, it sets our focus on what is in front of us and not behind us. It is not about what happened in my past. It is all about what God has for me in my future.

> *"No eye has seen, no ear has heard, and no mind has imagined*
> *what God has prepared for those who love him."*
> (1 CORINTHIANS 2:9 NLT)

HOPE COMES ALIVE WHEN WE TRULY BELIEVE THAT
GOD'S WORDS ABOUT US AND FOR US ARE TRUE.

This particular focus can be tricky. Here is why: if you don't believe there is hope in your future, then you won't be able to see a way forward for your future self. Hope comes alive when we truly believe that God's words about us and for us are true. The words of the song are true: "If you are not dead, He is not done."[11]

3) THE NEXT GENERATION

Envisioning our future selves will only get us so far. There are battles that we fight, prayers we pray, companies we build, and habits we break, knowing we will never fully enjoy the fruit of our labor. We are fighting, praying, building, and breaking for the next generation. Next-generation thinking was once common. As Americans, we have famous quotes from our founders about fighting a war so their great, great-grandchildren could be poets.[12] As Christians, we have an example of a God who is generational in His thinking, linking Abraham, Isaac, and Jacob. History is full of stories of immigrants who sacrificed everything so that their kids and grandkids could have a better future. Maybe your mom or dad or grandpa did without so you could go to college or have a chance to fulfill your dreams. Unfortunately, it seems that in the midst of self-seeking culture, the next generation is most often used as a prop for what we already want to happen instead of a reason to do difficult things today.

If we want to be people who live on, who don't quit, we must leverage the real power of the next generation as a motivator to dream, pray, build and break bigger and better. What does that look like? Imagine building a church. I'm not just talking about building the organization but even building the actual building. I can build it as cheap as possible and have what I need for today, or I can build with tomorrow in mind. How long do I want that building to stand? What difficulties do I want to take care of on behalf of the next generation? Do I want them to gripe every time they think of my efforts, or do I want them to cheer because they are standing on a firm foundation? When we build strong, we become a blessing to the next generation.

There is a famous picture of a large southern home on the Oak Alley Plantation. At the end of this row of gorgeous oak trees that create the most exquisite canopy stands a white house with columns. It is the perfect width of the trees. And when captured just right, the view is breathtaking. One would think that the house was built for the trees. It wasn't. Instead, an unknown French planter placed 28 seedlings in two even rows near his small home. He never saw them grow into their splendor. He must have known he never would. Yet, he planted anyway.[13]

That is what living on looks like. We keep going; we keep planting; we keep dreaming; we keep believing even when we don't know if we will enjoy the fruits of our labor.

As Christ-followers, our responsibility to the next generation is explicit. Our God is a generational God. The Bible says in Genesis that He is the God of Abraham, Isaac, and Jacob. We see life in terms of one life span; God sees life in terms of generations across time. His vision is not limited to what you accomplish in your lifetime. Rather, He sees what can be accomplished across the generations. He does not just have a plan for you. Instead, He has a plan that we have the chance to fit into. Your life isn't the whole chain; it's simply a link.

We see this most clearly in what some call the Hall of Fame of Faith: *It was by faith that Abraham obeyed when God called him to leave home and go to another land that God would give him as his inheritance. He went without knowing where he was going. And even when he reached the land God promised him, he lived there by faith—for he was like a foreigner, living in tents. And so did Isaac and Jacob, who inherited the same promise. Abraham was confidently looking forward to a city with eternal foundations, a city designed and built by God.*

It was by faith that even Sarah was able to have a child, though she was barren and was too old. She believed that God would keep his promise. And so a whole nation came from this one man who was as good as dead—a nation with so many people that, like the stars in the sky and the sand on the seashore, there is no way to count them.

All these people died still believing what God had promised them.
They did not receive what was promised, but they saw it all from
a distance and welcomed it. They agreed that they were foreigners
and nomads here on earth. Obviously people who say such things are
looking forward to a country they can call their own. If they had longed
for the country they came from, they could have gone back. But they
were looking for a better place, a heavenly homeland. That is why God
is not ashamed to be called their God, for he has prepared a city for
them. (Hebrews 11:8-16 NLT)

This scripture describes what it looks like to live a life that leaves a legacy of faith through the generations.

IF WE WANT TO EXPERIENCE THE EXTRAORDINARY, WE MUST FIRST WALK AWAY FROM THE ORDINARY.

The story of Abraham teaches us that we have to be willing to walk away from the familiar to find a new way of living. If we want to experience the extraordinary, we must first walk away from the ordinary. My ancestors were immigrants. They bravely walked away from their ordinary to find a new life. And today, their choices live on in me. What we choose to walk away from and walk toward will live on in the lives of our children through the generations. And that takes courage.

Courage is required for a life that lives on because fear does not fight fair. Fear is always doing its best to eliminate courage so we will not take the first step of faith. The first step will give us what we need to take the second: confidence. And confidence is what Abraham needed because even when he walked into his miracle, he lived by faith. If we just have courage to leave, we will find the confidence to stay. We can look back and say, "God was with me in the storm. So, He will be with me in the calm. He was with me when I pioneered. He will be with me as I settle here, too."

Abraham had the courage to walk away from his father's family and all that was familiar, and in the midst, he found he had the confidence to stay in that land, too. Some people have the courage to leave and journey, but they don't allow that courage to translate into confidence, faith to stay the course. When we have as our habit living on, then it will not matter whether it is the fear of the beginning, the boredom of the middle, or the doubts of the end, we will not quit.

Life does not always look the way that we thought it would. And it is in those moments that we must draw on courage and confidence to declare:

- I believe that His Word is true
- I believe that He will finish the work that He began in me
- I believe that He is able to fulfill His promises

IT IS IN THE STILLNESS THAT GOD TEACHES US THE COMPOSURE WE WILL NEED FOR THE LONG TERM.

Abraham and Sarah found themselves waiting a long time for their promise. I hate waiting. Sometimes, I will drive the long way around just to avoid sitting in traffic for the same amount of time. Standing still is difficult. Any kind of movement is preferable. And yet, it is in the stillness that God teaches us the composure we will need for the long term. It is that composure that our children and grandchildren see and remember.

How do we keep poised under pressure? How do we keep calm and carry on when facing confusion? Proverbs teaches us:

"Trust in the Lord with all your heart; do not depend on your own understanding. Seek his will in all you do, and he will show you which path to take." (Proverbs 3:5-6 NLT)

This sentiment is repeated by Paul when he is writing to the Philippians. "Don't worry about anything; instead, pray about everything. Tell God what you need, and thank him for all he has done. Then you will experience God's peace, which exceeds anything we can understand. His peace will guard your hearts and minds as you live in Christ Jesus" (Philippians 4: 6–7 NLT).

Trust is defined as the "firm belief in the reliability, truth, ability, or strength of someone or something."[14] Paul and David are both telling us that we must have a firm belief in the reliability of God, the truth of God, the ability of God, and the strength of God to truly follow Him and experience the abundant life.

The bottom line is this: when we pray and trust, then we experience God's peace. The scripture in Hebrews tells us that Sarah trusted God. Isaac, the promise, literally lived on because of Sarah's willingness not to quit, not to give up, and to trust God. She found peace in her heart in the midst of the wait. She would die before Isaac found a wife and gave her grandchildren. She would not see the complete fulfillment of the words God had spoken. God told Abraham and Sarah they would be father and mother to many generations. Sarah only saw one son. Yet she trusted God. The next generation is not merely the replacement squad. We should not look at succession as replacement. Rather, succession, the next generation, is about seeing the promise from afar.

Hebrews tells us that "All these people [heroes of the faith] died still believing what God had promised them. They did not receive what was promised, but they saw it all from a distance and welcomed it" (Hebrews 11:13 NLT). The Message translation says that they waved to the promise from afar. I can see Sarah dying in faith, still waving at the generations that would come. God's promise was bigger than what she could see. She lived a life that continues to live on.

When we determine to live on despite what we see, we can see our dreams and hopes live on in the next generation. We can welcome the promise from a distance even when we do not see it come to pass ourselves. Life is bigger than us. The choices of today, the fights of today, the victories of today have impacts far beyond what we can see and even beyond our lifetimes.

4) ETERNITY

Christ-followers believe that we are created eternal beings. That means God created our souls, the part of us that is most us, to live forever in eternity with Him. What we believe about eternity can be summed up very simply:

- ◆ Heaven is a real place
- ◆ God exists there in a way we can't experience Him here on earth
- ◆ You are invited, and you belong

HOW WE LIVE LIVES ON INTO ETERNITY

Our lives matter because they do not end in our physical death. How we live lives on into eternity. For the Christ-follower, entrance into heaven isn't a matter of good works or meeting certain standards. Instead, we rely on the sacrifice of Christ to cover our sins. This is what that means practically: when we accept Christ as Savior, He gives us the right to live eternally with Him in heaven. He also gives us the ability to live the abundant life here on earth.

There is more to eternity than just getting into heaven. Once there, the Bible teaches that our works here on earth will be judged and rewarded. What we do here matters. If we know that we will live on in eternity, we should take the challenge to not quit, to persist, to achieve our mission here on earth even more seriously.

Stopping and reminding yourself of the BIG picture, the eternal picture, helps us to live on and not quit. We are part of a much bigger story. Our future hasn't been written yet, but our life is not the end of OUR future. When we stand with all the generations together before God, our greatest hope will be that we did our part, stood our ground, and fought our good fight. We don't have to wait until then to have a perspective of eternity. We can choose to stop, be still, and remember.

QUITTING VS. STOPPING

STOPPING SOMETHING THAT IS NOT ADDING VALUE
TO YOUR LIFE OR NOT CONNECTED TO YOUR
MISSION CAN BE A STRATEGIC PART OF LIVING ON.

Let me be clear: "We live on" isn't really about whether you stay at your job, play your sport next season, or even keep the same set of friends. Instead, it is an overall choice not to quit on life, hope, your mission, and the core priorities of your life. See, you must live on even when your season of life changes, your employment changes, or even your relationships change. Jobs and involvement in community don't define this habit. Stopping something that is not adding value to your life or not connected to your mission can be a strategic part of living on. After all, we have limits and cannot do everything! Every Yes is really a No to something else. So, be strategic, but don't be hopeless.

We know the difference when we are quitting instead of stopping. Quitting is all emotion, comes from a place of failure or weakness, and makes us less excited about the future, not more. Strategic stopping is more like a change of direction. It can even lighten our load and give us more energy as we move to the next season of our lives. In fact, living on will require a lot of strategic stopping along the way. You will have to stop saying the things you used to say, using the coping mechanisms you used to use, leaning on the excuses you used to have, focusing on the problems you can't solve. You will also have to make strategic choices about what you will do rather than what you have to do.

See, nothing makes us want to quit more and steals our joy more efficiently than believing we have no choice. I can't quit because of my kids. I can't quit because I'm in charge. Those sound great but are self-defeating. They make you feel stuck and powerless. The truth is, you can do whatever you choose to do and pay the price for. Instead of being stuck, recognize the God-given power you have to choose the life you will live. "I will live on for my kids." "I choose to give my best to this leadership moment." "I can move forward into my next best." These are powerful statements that more accurately reflect reality. You do have a choice, and choosing to live on is a powerful habit that sets a foundation for every habit that is to come.

LIVING ON REQUIRES THE RIGHT FOUNDATIONS

Remember, it will be a choice to live on. We must live on over and over again until it becomes a habit. Living on will never be the result of a feeling. Living on must be a decision that is made, and often that decision will be made long before the storm arises. Paul reminds us in Galatians 6:9 (NLT), "So let's not get tired of doing what is good. At just the right time we will reap a harvest of blessing if we don't give up." Paul warns us not to get tired because it is easy to get tired and to quit. It is natural. It is understandable. No one is saying that if you are tired and want to give up, you are wrong or defective. No, Paul is urging us not to quit because more is waiting for us. If we do not live on, we will miss the harvest of blessing! If we don't give up, there is a reward coming.

If we want to live on through the frustrations of life, then we must make sure we have the right foundations. The question is: can your foundations handle your frustrations?

Living on means more than not quitting; it means building the right foundation by living on the right things. For a Christian, right is defined by the scriptures, specifically Christ's command to love others as He has loved us. Paul tells the Ephesians, a young church growing in the faith, "For we are God's masterpiece. He has created us anew in Christ Jesus, so we can do the good things he planned for us long ago" (Ephesians 2:10 NLT). We were literally created to do good things. Good things for who? For others! If you have ever served people, loved people, occupied your day with doing good for others, you know it can be tiring.

WE MUST BE COMMITTED TO LIVE ON, TO STAY THE COURSE, TO NOT QUIT, IN ORDER TO SEE THE BENEFITS IN THE LONG RUN.

In Galatians, Paul is telling us not to tire of doing good. When we are tired from doing bad and destructive things, that is another issue altogether! A life that lives on is built upon the right foundations of doing good works. Such a life, such a habit, takes time and commitment to build. Bad habits aren't easy to change. Good habits aren't easy to create. We must be committed to live on, to stay the course, to not quit, in order to see the benefits in the long run. Living on the right things gives us the strength for the race. What we live on will live on in us!

The Message paraphrase of the New Testament interprets Jesus' words in the gospel of Luke this way: "Why are you so polite with me, always saying 'Yes, sir,' and 'That's right, sir,' but never doing a thing I tell you? These words I speak to you are not mere additions to your life, homeowner improvements to your standard of living. They are foundation words, words to build a life on. If you work the words into your life, you are like a smart carpenter who dug deep and laid the foundation of his house on bedrock. When the river burst its banks and crashed against the house, nothing could shake it; it was built to last. But if you just use my words in Bible studies and don't work them into your life, you are like a dumb carpenter who built a house but skipped the foundation. When the swollen river came crashing in, it collapsed like a house of cards. It was a total loss" (Luke 6:46–49).

The question is whether we are working the words of God into our lives so that when the storm comes, we can live on because of what we have chosen to live on day in and day out. We don't want to just use His words as Bible studies or to make ourselves feel better or superior. No! Instead, we want to allow the scriptures to change us from the inside out and to teach us how to live on despite adversity, difficulty, and challenge.

///

FOR A CHRIST-FOLLOWER, WE HAVE SHARED TRUTHS, CONVICTIONS, AND TESTIMONY THAT DRIVES US FORWARD TO LIVE ON AND NOT QUIT.

\\

Those who have the habit of living on, who do not quit, tend to live on, intentionally fill their lives with the same things: truth, convictions, testimony.

- Truth is what you have decided to make the core of your life. This is the non-negotiable part of your existence—your big-picture worldview.
- Convictions or beliefs are what you understand to be true today. They can change, but so long as you hold them, you follow them. They are the leadings of today—the way that truth works out into our lives.
- Testimony is the story you tell about yourself and the world around you. It is the way in which you make sense of your existence. And it is the stories that you rehearse that will become the foundation of your life.

For a Christ-follower, we have shared truths, convictions, and testimony that drives us forward to live on and not quit.

LIVE ON THE TRUTH OF CHRIST

So now you Gentiles are no longer strangers and foreigners. You are citizens along with all of God's holy people. You are members of God's family. Together, we are his house, built on the foundation of the apostles and the prophets. And the cornerstone is Christ Jesus himself. We are carefully joined together in him, becoming a holy temple for the Lord. Through him you Gentiles are also being made part of this dwelling where God lives by his Spirit. (Ephesians 2:19-22 NLT)

Jesus told him, "I am the way, the truth, and the life. No one can come to the Father except through me." (John 14:6 NLT)

Jesus is the truth. When we build our lives on Christ, we build on the surest and truest foundation. Jesus Christ is the cornerstone of the Church, but He must also be the cornerstone of your life. Keep in mind that the cornerstone was around long before we were pouring concrete slabs for foundations. In Jesus' time, the foundations of buildings would have been laid with stone. The cornerstone concept is derived from the first stone set in the construction of a foundation. This would have been extremely important since all other stones would be set in reference to this one stone, thus determining the position of the entire structure.

> CHRISTIANITY REQUIRES US TO ALLOW GOD TO WRECK OUR FOUNDATION AND START BUILDING ANEW WITH CHRIST AS THE CORNERSTONE.

Keep in mind, Jesus isn't a stone in our foundation. He is *the* stone. He is the cornerstone that shapes the position of our entire lives. Jesus doesn't just impact our spiritual life. He sets the attitudes, actions, perspectives, and opinions of our whole lives. Jesus sets the position of your marriage, language, business, parenting, goals, and future. Christianity does not make sense when we simply try to add Jesus into our already established life. Christianity requires us to allow God to wreck our foundation and start building anew with Christ as the cornerstone.

When we set Christ as the cornerstone, we put ourselves in alignment with His power, peace, joy, provision, and plan. In essence, we get into alignment with the abundant life.

WE LIVE ON THE TRUTH OF OUR CONVICTIONS

If we live on the truth that is Christ, we must also live on the truth of Christ, our convictions.

Jesus said to the people who believed in him, "You are truly my disciples if you remain faithful to my teachings. And you will know the truth, and the truth will set you free." (John 8:31-32 NLT)

A conviction is simply a fixed or firm belief, the state of being convinced. Our convictions flow out of what we are convinced of. Sometimes, as Christ-followers, what we see and what we believe do not line up. In those moments, people say we have blind faith. I disagree; we have faith that lives on. We don't stop because, for the moment, things are unclear. We trust that God will continue to work in our lives despite what we see. Paul writes to the Corinthians and does not tell them to shut their eyes but rather to live based on what they are convinced of rather than what they see around them. "For we live by faith, not by sight" (2 Corinthians 5:7 NIV). If we want to live on, we can't live by what we see but rather by what we are convinced is true.

Doubts do not scare God. And we should feel free to bring our questions to the one who has all the answers. Questions can create clarity. They build on truth to help me create better convictions on which to live. We bring our questions through prayer, study of God's words, and connecting with community. Incredible courses like Alpha Course are intentionally designed to help answer the big questions of Christianity. One thing I love to remember is that our faith is 2,000 years old. Any question I have has been asked before. It's up to me to find the paths others have walked towards God's truth and find peace in the midst of my own path.

OUR BELIEFS, WHAT WE KNOW TO BE TRUE, MUST TAKE PRECEDENCE OVER OUR FEELINGS AND LEAD OUR BEHAVIORS.

We dedicate all our energy to our doubts. Our doubts are shaky ground, not strong enough to build a life on. Doubts keep us focused on our fears. Allowing our doubts to drive us toward Christ, toward deeper understanding, is healthy and good. We can use those doubts to shore up our foundations. Where we find our doubts simply creating feelings of unhappiness and uncertainty without action, we know they are hurting rather than helping us grow. We cannot live on our feelings, even if understanding our feelings is important. In other words, we should listen to our feelings but not allow them to lead us. Our beliefs, what we know to be true, must take precedence over our feelings and lead our behaviors. When we live on our convictions, base our decisions on our convictions, allow those convictions to strengthen us, allow our doubts to force us to clarify and shape our convictions, we will build a life that lives on through the storm.

WE LIVE ON THE TRUTH OF OUR TESTIMONY

All Christ-followers have a testimony of grace; this is our story of how we fit into God's story. And it is that testimony that allows us to live on past yesterday's struggles into what God has for us tomorrow.

And they have defeated him by the blood of the Lamb and by their testimony. And they did not love their lives so much that they were afraid to die. (Revelation 12:11 NLT)

We don't win on our own. We aren't forgiven by our deeds. We will never earn our salvation. We have a testimony of grace because it is by grace through faith that we have been saved. Sometimes, we can forget how important it is to remember our own testimony. Christ's victory is personal for each of us. It is by grace through faith that each of us has been saved (Ephesians 2:8). When we take time to recount our own grace testimony, we find the strength to live on in spite of the challenges surrounding us.

Not only do we have a testimony of grace, but we also have testimonies of God's greatness. King David, a man God called "after his own heart," understood the power of talking about what God had done in the past in the middle of today's trial.

Has the Lord rejected me forever?
Will he never again be kind to me?

Is his unfailing love gone forever?
Have his promises permanently failed?
Has God forgotten to be gracious?
Has he slammed the door on his compassion?
And I said, "This is my fate;
the Most High has turned his hand against me."
But then I recall all you have done, O Lord;
I remember your wonderful deeds of long ago. (PSALM 77:7-11 NLT)

When discouraged, we must remember God's faithfulness in the past. We must remember, as David says, His "wonderful deeds of long ago." Our testimony is bigger than our own personal story. We are part of a huge living book of testimonies that stretch back to the beginning of time. The testimonies of God's faithfulness in the Bible will encourage us and remind us of His greatness. The stories of how God has used ordinary men and women throughout history to make a difference can show us that we are not too far gone to be used by Him.

SURROUND YOURSELF WITH THE STORIES, THE TESTIMONIES, OF WHO GOD IS AND WHAT HE HAS DONE.

Surround yourself with the stories, the testimonies, of who God is and what He has done. Read biographies of the great men and women of past generations. Ask questions of those in your own community who have experienced God's faithfulness. Tell your kids and friends about what God has done in your own life. When we live on testimonies, make them part of our everyday existence, we find strength for the everyday challenges that we all face. We find the strength to live on.

WE LIVE ON IN COMMUNITY

Choosing not to quit is much easier when surrounded by others cheering you to the goal line. Researchers at Kansas State University found that when you work out with others, you push yourself harder and go further than when you work out alone.[15] Why? Because community encourages us to live on. Isolation is a major factor in suicide. Isolation is a major factor in all kinds of mental illnesses. The Covid-19 pandemic showed many of us that when isolated for long periods of time, we eventually experience all sorts of negative emotions and yearn for human contact. Why? Because God created you and me to live *in* community.

So many Christians today feel church is an outdated concept. The truth is, they aren't criticizing church as much as methodology. Church is the community of Christians who are living out their common beliefs and convictions together. If we ever think we are strong enough to stand alone, we should remember the example of our Savior. Jesus chose to live in community on this earth. And we should follow His example because we are Christ-followers.

The apostle Paul understood the importance of living and practicing faith within a community. In one of his many letters, he challenges the church at Thessaloniki, saying, "Therefore encourage one another and build each other up, just as in fact you are doing" (1 Thessalonians 5:11 NIV). Paul is reminding the church that they are doing more than just "hanging out," they are creating an atmosphere of encouragement and strength. You may not realize it, but you are encouraging those around you simply by showing up, being faithful, and being a part of the community.

WE FIND STRENGTH AND COURAGE IN THE STORIES AND STRUGGLES AND TRIUMPHS OF OTHERS.

It is easier to choose to live on instead of quitting when those around you are encouraging you. We find strength in our shared battles, shared joys, shared experiences. We hear the stories of those around us and are encouraged that we, too, can overcome the present challenge. When Destiny was going through a particularly difficult season, one of our pastors encouraged her to share the current challenge before there had been any breakthrough. Victory stories in church are common, but how often do we get to see the struggle in the middle? So, she stood on our stage and said, "It is okay to struggle. It is not okay to quit." We were surprised to find that of all the truths and victories we had shared, this testimony of weakness gave strength to so many. Why? Because everyone can identify with struggle. Not everyone can identify with success. The most common of pains can unite us in strength when we are just honest. The bottom line is we are created to live on in community. We find strength and courage in the stories and struggles and triumphs of others.

Your example of living on despite having every reason to quit will impact those around you and give them strength to not quit in the midst of their own struggles.

We live on.

Say it Again:

- If we cannot live through the tragedy of today, then we will never experience the triumph of tomorrow.
- Living on means choosing in advance not to quit on the mission.
- Living on is a reality as a created being:
  - › As eternal beings, we will live on past death into eternity.
  - › Our decisions have an impact on the next generation. Our lives live on in them through our good and bad choices.
- Living on also means choosing to build our lives on the right things. As a believer, we should build our lives on:
  - › The truth of Christ
  - › The truth of our convictions
  - › Our own experiences with Christ—our testimony
  - › Christian community
- When we make a habit to live on, not to quit, and to live on the right things, then our lives live on through the promises and goodness of God down through the generations.

Make it Personal:

- What do you live on daily? What inputs drive your life, your mood, your decisions? Are they what you want to live on, build on for the future? What needs to change?
- Write down three things you'd like to be said about you after you are gone from this earth or this job or even this community. Do your current priorities ensure that these will be the things that live on after you are gone?
- What dreams are you investing in that will be too big to finish in your lifetime?
- Who, in the next generation, are you investing in on a regular basis?

HABIT TWO

WE LOVE BIG

Darkness cannot drive out darkness; only light can do that.
Hate cannot drive out hate; only love can do that.
—Martin Luther King, Jr.

So now I am giving you a new commandment: Love each other.
Just as I have loved you, you should love each other. Your love for
one another will prove to the world that you are my disciples.
—Jesus

Love is big business these days. And everyone has their own definition. When we chose this habit, we weren't thinking of the ubiquitous Valentine's balloons, personal preferences, or even the conditional love of a fickle public. Instead, we had in mind the kind of love that makes no sense to us and defines an eternal God.

"For God so loved the world that he gave his one and only Son, that
whoever believes in him shall not perish but have eternal life."
(John 3:16 NIV)

The core of the gospel is love. It is not our love for God but God's love for us that defines the gospel story (1 John 4:10). God so loved the world that He gave Jesus as a sacrifice in our place. We were separated from God, and God stepped in the gap because He SO loved. In our house and in our church, we often say, *so* love is *big* love. And we love big.

Big love is a mandate of scripture. Jesus tells us, "A new command I give you: Love one another. As I have loved you, so you must love one another. By this everyone will know that you are my disciples, if you love one another" (John 13:34–35). Jesus was saying something *new*! His kingdom wouldn't be defined by the millions of do's and don'ts of the law. Instead, it would be defined by the actions that we each take toward each other. It is not an option to love big; it is *the* command of the gospel.

LOVE IS A MINDSET

BIG LOVE ISN'T JUST A SET OF ACTIONS, IT IS A MINDSET.

Our mindset is our established set of attitudes. Our attitude is our settled way of thinking or feeling about someone or something. So, it could be said that our mindset is a collection of settled ways of thinking or feeling about the world. Big love isn't just a set of actions, it is a mindset. And if we want to love people like God loves us, then we have to cultivate the mindset of God about humanity.

The writer of the book of First John understood the importance of receiving the love we give to others from God. He writes to his fellow Christ-followers, "Dear friends, let us continue to love one another, for love comes from God. Anyone who loves is a child of God and knows God. But anyone who does not love does not know God, for God is love." Love comes from God. Does that mean we stand around and wait for love to download from on high? No, but we must take on the mindset of God in order to love like God.

Our mindset comes from our beliefs which form our identity. It could be said that our mindset is a reflection of that identity. Researchers like

Dr. Carol Dweck have shown that beliefs about whether or not you can improve at a given task actually translate into whether or not you do improve at a given task. Likewise, our beliefs about others have a real-world impact on them.[16]

These beliefs can be identified and changed if we are willing to go through the pain of confronting ourselves. You might think it isn't worth it. Yet Christ went through so much pain to bridge the gap for us so that we could experience His love. Shouldn't we be willing to endure the discomfort of change to love others the way God loves us?

I am a bit of an introvert. Actually, I test as the most extreme introvert on the scale. When I was fourteen, I realized that while I was comfortable sitting with my two friends at lunch, speaking to no one, and keeping my head down and doing my work, that behavior was not going to allow me to impact the world. So, with sweaty palms, I began the hard work of changing my behavior and mindset about how to speak to, engage with, and care for others. It has been a lifelong process. Most people who know me now as pastor or coach wouldn't know that I actually prefer to be alone.

One of the deep beliefs I have had to overcome on the way to loving big is, "They don't care if I show up." I assumed that my presence didn't matter to others. So, over and over again, I wouldn't show up. It was only when Destiny convinced me that loving big requires me to show up that I confronted that belief and started changing my mindset. I was a person who was willing to come if you called and had an emergency. Now, I am a person who looks for ways to love big by showing up at important moments. What changed? My belief and, therefore, my mindset.

PEOPLE ARE VALUABLE BECAUSE GOD HAS PLACED THE HIGHEST VALUE ON THEM.

Another belief that can impact your ability to love big is, "It's just not worth it." People can be difficult. Life can be hard. And often, you receive nothing back when you choose to love those around you in a big way. So, why is it worth it? Loving big is worth it because it is worth it to God. We love as a reflection of His love toward us and His influence over our lives. Yet, even the right actions will be tainted with the wrong attitude if you don't confront that belief. A "they aren't worth it" mindset is often accompanied by an "I'm the only sane person on the planet" identity. People are valuable because God has placed the highest value on them. We each have issues and blind spots just like everyone else. To love big, we must align our beliefs with God's beliefs about ourselves and humanity and allow those beliefs to change our identity and our mindset.

Think for a moment about your beliefs about people in your life or humanity in general that keep you from loving big. Can you name them? Write down the thoughts that come to mind and then begin to investigate what God says about humanity. He loves us big. So, we can love others big, too.

We love big intentionally by filling in the gaps. We have determined in our city to be gap fillers. When we realize that some outreach we are doing is already being done better by someone else, we stop and join in with them. And we are constantly on the outlook for true gaps where no one is leaning in. In the midst of need is the greatest opportunity to love big. It is difficult without volunteer coordinators, pretty job descriptions, or clear deliverables. Yet, gaps are exactly where I think God lives, waiting for us to join Him in loving the world big.

"We Love Big!" has become a unifying cry for our home and our church. It takes away the hesitant approach to loving a world that God went to extreme measures to reach. If God so loved us, how can we do anything else but love each other big? After all, the scriptures say that our love for each other is the greatest testimony that we are His kids. Shouldn't we, of all people, be known for really big love?

SO, WHY DON'T WE LOVE BIG?

If we look at our reality, we know that loving big isn't exactly what Christians are known for. Sure, it is one of the things that some Christian groups like Samaritan's Purse or the Salvation Army are known for. However, it is far from the identifying mark Christ intended our love to be. Why is that? We can rail against the choices of others, shake our heads at the difficulty of large-scale change, or we can start with the one person we can control—ourselves. Why don't we love big? Here are three hurdles everyone must constantly climb over to love the way Jesus loved.

OUR DIFFERENCES

We are all quite different. I can look at my five children and see a microcosm of the immense diversity of humanity even in the midst of the same home. One child is introverted, another the class clown, still another a serious student, and another a constantly moving athlete. They share a home, parents, language, religion, and yet there are differences. And those differences cause conflict!

Extrapolate that microcosm of difference across your neighborhood, across your city, across your country, across the globe, and we can see a serious hurdle to loving big.

Some differences are hard to see. Others are right on the surface. When we judge people in advance based on their skin color, nationality, language, ethnicity, we are choosing to focus on what makes us different instead of valuing what we share in common. Prejudice—literally pre-judging—is an affront to every single thing that Christ died for. It is antithetical to the gospel, which declares a new allegiance and brotherhood higher than any other.

WE KNOW THAT NATURALLY IT IS EASIER TO LOVE
WHAT WE UNDERSTAND AND WHAT IS FAMILIAR.

We know that naturally it is easier to love what we understand and what is familiar. It's easier to be prejudiced against outsiders when you have not experienced what it is to be an outsider. Many who are harsh towards those of a lower socio-economic class have not themselves suffered the difficulties that come from not having enough. Yet it doesn't take much for us to find commonalities that allow us to see differences, well, differently.

I cannot imagine a greater difference between two individuals or groups than what exists between humanity and our God Creator. Not only is He divine, and we are mortal, but He is also holy, and we are imperfect. Unlike the surface differences that I listed earlier, the differences between God and us are differences that really matter. Yet, God sent Himself to us in full view of our differences. God loved past our differences because He placed a value on us. And He asks us to do the same.

When we start with the belief that every human is created in God's image and therefore worthy of our love and respect, it changes the way we see difference. It becomes strange that we would allow what is different to keep us apart or make us apathetic to the pain of our neighbors. After all, we have so much more in common. When we see everyone as loved by God, we are able to begin the journey of loving everyone as God loved us. Make no mistake: we don't love in spite of difference. We learn to love because of our differences. Love covers the gap.

What "kinds" of people do you feel less comfortable around? What differences create barriers to big love for you? How can you align your beliefs with God's to allow you to develop a big love mindset? These questions will help you determine how differences may be standing in the way of loving big.

OUR PREFERENCES

///

PROBLEMS OCCUR WHEN WE ELEVATE
OUR PREFERENCES OVER PEOPLE.

\\

Our differences often expose our preferences. There is nothing wrong with having preferences. In fact, those little quirks of personality and intellect make the world a more beautiful and colorful place. Problems occur when we elevate our preferences over people.

We each have theological preferences, takes on issues that are outside of the core principles of salvation and eternity. We may have political preferences or entertainment preferences, or even cultural preferences. The key is not to conform to the preferences of others but instead to love people over our own preferences.

If we are not careful, our preferences can separate us from those around us. We can start cultivating new groups of "others" who we can exclude from the call to love. You may prefer to sing different songs in your church than mine, or maybe you vote different than I do, but God's call is still the same: love BIG!

The difficulty comes when we are convinced that we are right! Our preference is the best way! I get it. I am naturally that way too. There is only one right way to live, drive, hang toilet paper. Everyone else is doing it WRONG! Destiny has helped to show me that there is a great variety of preferences that are neither right nor wrong; they are just preferences. What about the "preferences" that are central to what we really believe is best for us and even the world? We still cannot use them as an excuse not to love!

This requirement to love people over preferences is why we cannot participate in cancel culture, whether on the left, right, center, or fringe. Know what is important to you. Fight for what you believe in. Express truth even when it is inconvenient. At the same time, we must love those who don't share our preferences, beliefs, or truth. That means continuing to value them as human beings and inviting them to the table as God continues to invite us.

Remember that Jesus died for us while we were still sinners, far apart from Him. And He continues to walk with us even though our lives are far from the perfection that His way requires. He doesn't shun or cancel us when we don't live up to a standard or even when we choose to act against His way. Instead, He lovingly walks with us, and that journey changes us. When we choose to love past preferences, we have the chance to change our world but also to have our own lives changed in return.

OUR EXPERIENCES

Not only are our differences and preferences hurdles to loving big, but our experiences can also create beliefs that create a limiting mindset towards our neighbors. Our experiences are simply what we have been through, seen, and even how we were raised. Remember the first time you were truly disappointed? Do you recall the faces of those friends who betrayed you or that stranger who deceived you? Each of us has gone through something painful or unexpected, or difficult. The question is whether we will allow those events to cause us to lose trust and hope and ultimately keep us from loving those around us as Christ has loved us.

> OUR ANSWER TO THE PAIN OF THE PAST IS TO STOP OPENING OUR HEARTS TO THE FUTURE.

When we are hurt, sometimes we respond by believing that if we limit contact with others, we can prevent that same pain from occurring in the future. Our answer to the pain of the past is to stop opening our hearts to the future. And we can easily find ourselves choosing not to love big.

I'm grateful that after Jesus was rejected by friends and family alike, was criticized by so many, and even betrayed by one of His disciples, He didn't allow those experiences to keep Him from loving us. We are able to know God and follow the teachings of Christ today with the power of the Holy Spirit because Jesus didn't allow His experiences to keep Him from loving BIG!

So, once again, the question comes to whether we will choose Jesus' way or our own. Will we allow our experiences to keep us from loving others, or will we allow our experience with Christ to remind us to love others? I'm not minimizing what you have gone through. I am saying that the answer isn't to shut yourself away from the world. Instead, choose to continue to love the way that Jesus loves. Another way to say it would be to choose God's way of seeing humanity over your own experience-informed conclusions about humanity. He sees the full picture and yet He continues to love us. So, we can, in turn, choose to love others.

LOVE IS AN ACTION

Remember DC Talk's hit song *Love is a Verb*? You probably do not because it was a million years ago—90s Christianity at its best—so let me enlighten you. The message was simple but so true. The love of God demanded action, the sending of Jesus. To love like God, we will also have to take action. Christian love, big love, is not an emotion. It is not social media awareness. It is not a like on a Facebook page. It is not a nice word or sentiment thrown in at an appropriate time. It is much more and demands much more of each of us as Christ-followers.

The Bible seems to address the "I feel so bad about this issue, and now I've expressed it, so that is loving the world" attitude pervasive in our society today. James, the half-brother of Jesus and His devoted disciple made it clear that seeing a need and not taking action outside of words is worthless. "Suppose a brother or a sister is without clothes and daily food. If one of you says to them, 'Go in peace; keep warm and well fed,' but does nothing about their physical needs, what good is it?" (James 2:15–16 NIV). Then John, the self-proclaimed disciple whom Jesus loved, echoed the sentiment. "This is how we know what love is: Jesus Christ laid down His life for us. And we ought to lay down our lives for our brothers and sisters. If anyone has material possessions and sees a brother or sister in need but has no pity on them, how can the love of God be in that person? Dear children, let us not love with words or speech but with actions and in truth" (1 John 3:16–18 NIV).

The apostles, the leaders of the church, agreed with Jesus. Loving BIG means loving with actions, not just words. Big love is reflected in how we treat each other, not just how we feel about each other. Loving big has to become a habit.

BIG LOVE IS BOLD LOVE

Loving big requires us to be bold. When we choose to love big, we are choosing to throw proportion and rules out the window! After all, God loved even when we didn't have the capacity to love back. In fact, this continues to be true. He loves us even when we can't love back. Paul tells the Romans, "But God demonstrates his own love for us in this: While we were still sinners, Christ died for us" (Romans 5:8 NIV). This is disproportionate. It abandons the rules. It is not fair. And it is how God asks us to love others.

God changed the rules and took our punishment on Himself. He adopted us into His family. He gave us His name, His righteousness, His inheritance, His heart. And, it is clear through the gospels God has continued to love us even when we reject Him time and time again. I'm so grateful God's love has never given up on me! And if you don't think it is a miracle God still loves you, then maybe you should skip ahead to the habit of "We Practice Honesty."

LOVING BIG MEANS THAT WE LOVE THOSE WHO ARE DIFFICULT TO LOVE.

Loving big means that we love those who are difficult to love. I remember an event we held to give away school uniforms to families who could not afford to purchase them. A volunteer walked up to me furiously. "That woman was ungrateful! She didn't even smile or say anything!" I'm not sure what she wanted me to do at that moment.

Maybe she thought I'd march out there and give "that woman" a lecture or rip the uniforms from her child's arms. You may cringe at this woman's attitude, but how often does it reflect our own? We get angry with the child who doesn't understand our sacrifice. We keep track of the wrongs done to us by others, demanding an apology and restitution for every offense. We avoid speaking to, much less loving on, the annoying church member who always needs to talk.

Do we understand that big love, God's love, requires us to seek out and love with actions those who are difficult? Jesus makes it clear that is exactly what we are to do:

> You have heard the law that says, 'Love your neighbor' and hate your enemy. But I say, love your enemies! Pray for those who persecute you! In that way, you will be acting as true children of your Father in heaven. For he gives his sunlight to both the evil and the good, and he sends rain on the just and the unjust alike. If you love only those who love you, what reward is there for that? Even corrupt tax collectors do that much. If you are kind only to your friends, how are you different from anyone else? Even pagans do that. But you are to be perfect, even as your Father in heaven is perfect. (Matthew 5: 43-48 NLT)

THERE IS NEVER AN EXCUSE TO HATE AFTER WHAT JESUS HAS DONE FOR US.

Loving big requires we even love our enemies. There is never an excuse to hate after what Jesus has done for us. We love without fear simply because God asks us to do so. It has been said, "Us versus them is a false choice." For the Christ-follower, this is the core of how we are called to love. We love big because Jesus showed us the way and asked us to follow, not because we want resolution or a response. This is bold. And it should be. Christ boldly loved us. And we should boldly love each other.

BIG LOVE IS INTENTIONAL

They do not love that do not show their love.
—WILLIAM SHAKESPEARE

Loving big requires us to be intentional! Loving big, whether we are talking about our families or our communities, isn't something that just happens. It does not just naturally occur over time. No, loving big is a series of small intentional actions that accumulate into meaningful relationships. We have to choose to love big.

Once, when I (Destiny) was fighting with Phillip, I made the mistake of complaining to my grandmother. She listened to my story and then proceeded to tell me that I was not being a very good Christian. I felt that was beside the point. "Didn't God tell you to love your husband?" Well, yes, but Phillip was in the wrong. And then I realized his wrong didn't let me off the hook. When I choose the habit of loving big, loving as God loves, I have to love despite my circumstances, not because of my circumstances. I have to love intentionally, especially when I feel I have a right not to. And that obligation extends especially to my family, not to everyone but my family.

Loving big is a decision first and an emotion second, and it starts with our relationship with God. Jesus says, "If you love me, obey my commandments" (John 14:15 NLT). Being intentional to love big will require us to act out of our decisions rather than our emotions. You can't live a life of big love when your love is tied to your emotions. Love must be tied to decisions! Love must be a habit.

What does intentionally loving big look like in a practical sense? We choose to view others with the eyes of love. God saw the world and felt compassion. What do we see when we look at those around us? 1 Corinthians 13, one of the most popular Bible chapters, tells us that love is kind, patient, and believes the best. When we put on our love glasses, that is what we must see. We must see a world through kind eyes, patient eyes, and eyes that believe the best about everyone around us. Sometimes, it is hardest to keep those love lenses focused when it comes to those closest to us. And yet, the mandate of loving big starts at home! Next time you get close to losing it on your child, spouse, co-worker, client, or even your neighbor, remember to look with loving eyes.

PEOPLE ARE GOD'S HEART. AND HE HAS MADE TIME FOR US. WE MUST MAKE TIME FOR EACH OTHER.

We must also make time for others in our schedules. The truth for most of us is that if it is not on the schedule, it doesn't exist. In other words, there is an element of planning that is required when we want to be intentional. I think that goes for big love, too. If you don't make time to give the basket to the neighbors, it won't happen. If you don't schedule the date with your spouse, it won't happen. If you don't clear an evening to serve those less fortunate, it likely will not happen. And if we pack our days so full with tasks that there is no room for people, then we have chosen to live outside of God's will. People are God's heart. And He has made time for us. We must make time for each other.

Say it Again:

- Love is the core of the gospel message.
  - › God so loved the world that He gave His only son.
  - › Jesus gave one new command, "Love others the way I have loved you."
- Love is a mindset that comes from submitting our lives to Christ and His way.
- Love is an action—it is not just an emotion.
- Loving big requires us to be bold and intentional.

Make it Personal:

What does love mean to you?

- Read 1 Corinthians 13 and write down the adjectives that describe love. Do your actions toward others in your life today, this week, this month line up with those adjectives?
- How can you intentionally love your family big today?
- Choose one neighbor or co-worker. What can you do to love them big, on purpose?
- Where do intentional acts of love rank on your schedule? How can you begin to prioritize the new way of living Christ has given us?

WE PROTECT UNITY

Alone we can do so little. Together we can do so much.
—HELEN KELLER

*Every kingdom divided against itself will be ruined, and every
city or household divided against itself will not stand.*
—JESUS

Behold, how good and pleasant it is when brothers dwell in unity!
(PSALM 133:1 ESV)

UNITY CANNOT EXIST WITHOUT ACTIVE PROTECTION

Destiny is a persistent failure of a gardener. There are many reasons. Consistency would be a big one. She starts with a lot of motivation in the spring, and somewhere in June, the heat defeats the vision. Not enough water and too much neglect result in miserly harvests. Another reason is a family of adorable rabbits lives in our backyard. We could put up fences or drive them away, but with the exception of a rather pathetic tomato cage, we've done nothing to deter the cute little scavengers. Destiny's garden is a nice idea, but I'm not worried about it, and I'm unlikely to spend a lot of energy protecting it. It's just not that important to me.

Many times, we do not make the effort to protect unity because we don't really value unity.[17] Other times, it just takes too much energy. It's like a preacher said, "Christianity would be great if it weren't for all the people." How could we ever serve a God who gave all He had for a world that had rejected Him if we don't value those around us?

WHAT IS UNITY?

Unity can be defined as oneness or agreement. We must stay in agreement with Jesus in order to stay in unity with Him. That means agreeing with what He says about our lives, regardless of how we feel. It means staying in agreement with what He says about our future, regardless of what we see. And it means staying in agreement with what Jesus says about the world, even when we can't understand. If you have difficulty being unified with other Christ-followers, you likely have a problem with being unified with Christ, too.

Unity with Christ drives us to an ever-deeper realization of what God has done for us and what He wants to do through us. "Since God chose you to be the holy people he loves, you must clothe yourselves with tenderhearted mercy, kindness, humility, gentleness, and patience. Make allowance for each other's faults, and forgive anyone who offends you. Remember, the Lord forgave you, so you must forgive others. Above all, clothe yourselves with love, which binds us all together in perfect harmony" (Colossians 3:12–14 NLT). Clothe yourself with love. God is love. Many people know about the love of God, but how many of us live in it? If we want unity with others, we must stay connected to the love of God and allow that love to bind us together in perfect harmony.

Unity with Christ does not mean uniformity with other believers. We are still uniquely ourselves while unified with Christ. And the more we understand that Christ allows us space and delights in our created uniqueness, the more likely we are to make room for each other. If I do not feel judged, I am less likely to judge. If I know I have faults, I'm more likely to make allowances for yours. If I am aware of the offenses I cause, I'm less likely to blow up when you offend me. My unity with Christ gives me the perspective and confidence I need to protect my unity with others.

UNITY CAN BECOME ESPECIALLY PROBLEMATIC WHEN POINTS OF THEOLOGY ARE INVOLVED.

Unity can become especially problematic when points of theology are involved. How am I unified if I disagree with an element of how you worship or what you consider appropriate behavior? I have found that if I protect the unity we have around what we agree on, then I earn the place to discuss our disagreements. Humility will prompt me to trust the Holy Spirit to work in you and guide you to truth, just as I trust Him to guide me. And that is a point of agreement, unity, that I can hold on to regardless of our differences.

UNITY IS WORTH THE ENERGY IT TAKES TO PROTECT IT.

Unity is worth the energy it takes to protect it. Before we can appropriately protect unity, we must believe it is worth protecting. After all, we will not protect something that is not important to us. So, why should unity be important to us?

GOD COMMANDS UNITY

First, God commands it. The apostle Peter tells us, "Finally, all of you be like-minded [united in spirit], sympathetic, brotherly, kindhearted [courteous and compassionate toward each other as members of one household], and humble in spirit; and never return evil for evil or insult for insult [avoid scolding, berating, and any kind of abuse], but on the contrary, give a blessing [pray for one another's well-being, contentment, and protection]; for you have been called for this very purpose, that you might inherit a blessing [from God that brings well-being, happiness, and protection]" (1 Peter 3:8–9 AMP). The scripture makes it clear that we are ordered by God through the teaching of the apostles to be united in spirit as members of one household (brothers and sisters). The apostle does not stop there. He tells us not to respond to evil with evil. Now, for those of you following along closely, this means we should expect evil even from some of those who are our "family" in Christ. And, yet, protecting unity requires that we respond to evil with blessing. God is commanding us to protect unity even when there is a personal cost.

In Ephesians, the apostle Paul exhorts the newly formed church. "Therefore I, a prisoner for serving the Lord, beg you to lead a life worthy of your calling, for you have been called by God. . . . Make every effort to keep yourselves united in the Spirit, binding yourselves together with peace" (Ephesians 4:1, 3 NLT). Living a life worthy of our calling isn't about writing books, speaking on stage, or even creating amazing art or businesses. Rather, it is making every effort to keep ourselves united in the Spirit.

UNITY IS GOD'S IDEA, AND HE DOES NOT JUST SUGGEST IT. HE DEMANDS IT FROM EACH OF US.

Every effort is an active and purposeful phrase. We are to bind ourselves together with peace according to the scriptures. This is active imagery and evokes a process that may at times be uncomfortable or even troublesome. The good news is unity isn't just your pastor's idea or your spouse's idea, or my idea. Unity is God's idea, and He does not just suggest it. He demands it from each of us.

Of course, there is a silver lining. God blesses those who protect unity. When we protect unity and make every effort to stay unified, we are not just wrapping our relationships in peace; we are wrapping our own hearts in peace. And I cannot think of a better reward than living a truly peaceful life.

JESUS DEMONSTRATED UNITY

Second, unity is important because Jesus demonstrated it through His earthly life. In the story of the Good Samaritan, Jesus asks, "Now which of these three would you say was a neighbor to the man who was attacked by bandits?" The man replied, "The one who showed him mercy." Then Jesus said, "Yes, now go and do the same" (Luke 10:36–37 NLT). This is not just a story. No, this was the life Jesus lived.

Jesus lived a life of loving big and protecting unity. He reached out to those who were disenfranchised and marginalized and brought them back into the center of His love and life. Imagine, this is the Savior who spoke to a Samaritan woman, alone, at the well. Jews like Jesus did not speak to Samaritans and normally not to women. Both were considered less valuable in some way, possibly contaminated in others. Yet, Jesus went out of His way, not only to speak to her, but to record the conversation for us. He pulled Matthew, the tax collector, into His inner circle. Everyone knew tax collectors were collaborating crooks in solidarity with the oppressors. Jesus seemed not to notice and invited Matthew anyway. He touched unclean men with leprosy and even issued His last earthly invitation to a thief condemned to die beside Him. And He talks to you, sees you, and invites you too.

> UNITY MEANS WE FOCUS ON WHAT WE HAVE IN COMMON RATHER THAN WHAT SEPARATES US.

None of these people, including you, were anything like Jesus. We can often mistake the call to unity as the call to uniformity. We feel that people have to become like us to belong. Protecting unity doesn't mean we vote the same, look the same, eat the same, talk the same, or even listen to the same music. Unity means we focus on what we have in common rather than what separates us. And we love each other because Jesus loves us.

You won't hear many conversations about politics in our church foyer. We've learned that to protect unity, we need to focus on what we have in common and create safe spaces to discuss our differences. I love hearing about dinners between groups in the church who come from different backgrounds or perspectives. I love hearing about the conversations that ensue, stories that are shared, common ground that is found. I want our church and my home to look like a church Jesus would attend, where everyone is welcome, and everyone belongs. Jesus demonstrated what it was to protect unity, not so we could just read about it, but so we could live it, too.

MISSION REQUIRES UNITY

The third reason unity is important is that our mission requires it. None of us want to fail. Some of us are more focused on winning or succeeding than others. I am 100 percent motivated by winning. Maybe you are too. Good news: unity is required to succeed at this mission. And winning is defined in the Christian context as advancing and expanding the Kingdom of God on the earth, our mission. We have an assignment to win! We have a mission to complete. And that mission requires unity even when there is no hope for uniformity.

Jesus knew the battle for unity would define Christianity. Could we stay unified despite our differences? John records Jesus as praying this way to His Father in heaven. "I have given them the glory you gave me, so they may be one as we are one. I am in them and you are in me. May they experience such perfect unity that the world will know that you sent me and that you love them as much as you love me" (John 17:22–23 NLT). Once again, Jesus tells us how important unity is to the mission. Our unity testifies to the validity of the truth that we declare. There is good news. Jesus saves! God transforms! There is abundant life! And if people can see this abundant life through the unity of the believers, we make it easier for them to see the God we are all unified around.

GOD IS LOOKING FOR OBEDIENCE, NOT PERFECTION.

Remember, unity with others starts with staying connected to Christ. Jesus uses the metaphor of a grapevine in John to explain how essential our unity with Him is to our lives together. "I am the vine; you are the branches. If you remain in me and I in you, you will bear much fruit; apart from me you can do nothing. If you do not remain in me, you are like a branch that is thrown away and withers; such branches are picked up, thrown into the fire and burned" (John 15:5–6 NIV). The difference between bearing fruit, much fruit, and being discarded as useless is our connection with Christ. God is looking for obedience, not perfection. We move forward. There is a process to progress. And all the while, we stay connected to Christ.

Protecting is active, not passive. In crafting these House Habits, we intentionally did not say "be unified." That wording is too passive. Instead, we used the word "protect" because it is active. Protecting requires me to be more than passively compliant; it requires action! Because it is a habit, I tell myself that in every situation, I will respond in a way that protects unity. Protecting unity becomes another lens through which I judge my actions.

HOW DO WE PROTECT UNITY?

First, take responsibility. The Bible tells us, "Do not repay anyone evil for evil. Be careful to do what is right in the eyes of everyone. If it is possible, as far as it depends on you, live at peace with everyone" (Romans 12:17–18 NIV). Unity will start with me. If I leave unity up to someone else, I'm setting myself up to lose.

I CANNOT PLEASE EVERYONE, BUT I MUST TAKE INTO ACCOUNT THE VIEW OF OTHERS AND CHOOSE EMPATHY.

Unity is my responsibility. And I'm responsible to see every situation from different perspectives. I'm not allowed to just say, "Well, I wouldn't be upset" or "I don't see what the big deal is." I'm required to think about how others see the situation and do what is right, not only in my eyes but in theirs, to the greatest extent possible. Expanding your view will often change what you believe is the right thing to do and the right way to respond. That may mean being sensitive in situations where I don't want to be sensitive. It means apologizing even when I've done nothing wrong. I cannot please everyone, but I must take into account the view of others and choose empathy.

Remember, the scripture says, "as far as it depends on you." It does not all depend on you. However, some of it does. Make sure that you are doing your best to live at peace, to protect unity. You cannot make peace with everyone, but you can make peace with someone. Unity is my responsibility. And when I take responsibility, I am empowered to protect it.

Second, ask questions. Communication helps foster unity. Lack of communication cripples unity. Communication brings deeper understanding, and understanding is a bridge to unity. Make a habit of protecting unity by asking questions first and making statements later.

"What did you mean when you said. . ."

"I am hearing you say. . . is that correct?"

"Tell me more about. . ."

These phrases allow us to gain awareness, not just spout our own answers. People rarely care about your opinion, but they do need to know you care about them. This is the secret: I don't have to agree with you to accept you. I don't have to defend my views to listen to yours. I can ask questions without drawing conclusions. The question is, am I willing to lay down my opinion and pick up some questions for the sake of unity? The more I understand you, the stronger our unity will be.

Third, give grace. If you want to protect unity, you will have to learn to give grace. Unity is best protected when we choose to give people the benefit of the doubt, believe the best in them, and determine that we will give grace no matter what. The apostle Paul instructs us to do just that. "Always be humble and gentle. Be patient with each other, making allowance for each other's faults because of your love" (Ephesians 4:2 NLT). When I choose to protect unity, I am choosing to be patient and make allowances for others. It is not about me being right or wrong. It is about our relationship and protecting what is most important, our unity.

As a church, we've decided that we will take responsibility, ask questions, and give grace when problems arise. We have made a habit of protecting unity. And the same process applies in our homes, our businesses, and our schools. When we choose to stay unified with Christ, He empowers us to protect the unity we have with each other.

About Destiny's garden. In 2021, I decided that maybe I should join her in the pursuit of home-grown vegetables. Actually, she was in her third trimester and decided to plant a full garden anyways. She is nothing if not persistent! So, it fell to me to begin watering the garden every single day. The harvest was incredible. We had so many cucumbers and okra and tomatoes. Our kids were thrilled. I am now hooked, and together we are plotting a winter garden for the first time. It's amazing what we can achieve together.

Say it Again:

- Unity is important to God. And because it is important to Him, it should be important to us.
- Unity cannot exist without active protection.
- Jesus demonstrated unity while He was here on earth.
- Our mission will require us to be unified as Christ-followers.
- We protect unity by:
  - › Taking responsibility for our own part in preserving unity.
  - › Asking questions first rather than making judgments.
  - › Giving grace.

Make it Personal:

- Why is unity important? Does unity mean uniformity?
- What prevents you from embracing the habit of protecting unity?
- How would you evaluate your connection with Christ? Are you staying unified with Him even when it means submitting your own opinion to His Lordship?
- How does staying connected with Christ help you to be unified with other believers?
- How can you practically take more responsibility for unity in your relationships?
- Where are you making statements and not asking questions?
- Where are you demanding grace but giving little?
- Ask God to search your heart and give you a passion for protecting what is important to Him—unity.

WE HONOR CONSISTENTLY

Humility forms the basis of honor, just as the low ground
forms the foundation of a high elevation.
—BRUCE LEE

True honor is an outflow from a heart that fears God.
—JOHN BEVERE

Don't forget to show hospitality to strangers, for some who have
done this have entertained angels without realizing it!
(HEBREWS 13:2 NLT)

What comes to your mind when you think about the word "honor"? Is it a medal that hangs on someone's neck? Is it a special place to sit or opportunity given in exchange for good service? Is it an award won for some great discovery or advancement? The Biblical idea of honor encompasses all that and so much more. Yes, we should give honor to those who deserve it. Yes, we should honor certain people like our parents or authorities because of their position in our lives. Yet, as in every aspect of life, Jesus asks for more! He asks us to honor everyone around us, consistently, as image bearers, those made in the likeness of God.

WHAT WE HONOR REFLECTS WHAT WE VALUE.

What we honor reflects what we value. To honor the Jesus way, we must lay a foundation for choosing God's ways and His values over our own. The first step to living a life that honors consistently is to place God at the center of our lives, and honor Him.

HONOR GOD

If we want to honor God, we will have to choose His ways over our own. Disobedience and sin are big words with a lot of baggage for many people. They are actually simple concepts. Disobedience and sin for the Christ-follower come down to choosing our own way over God's way. Jesus said it this way, "If you love me, keep my commands." What commands? In this particular passage, Jesus is talking about the command to believe in Him as God and as one who can be found by those who seek Him. The writer of Hebrews said it this way: "[W]ithout faith it is impossible to please God, because anyone who comes to him must believe that he exists and that he rewards those who earnestly seek him." Before you ever try to implement Jesus' way, you must believe in Jesus. Honoring God comes down to believing in Him first and then choosing His way every day.

How can we possibly overcome our own desires to do life our own way? Jesus didn't just say to keep his commands. He also promised that as we choose to keep His commands, live our lives His way, that He would send a comforter, the Holy Spirit, to guide us. The power of the Christian life comes from allowing the Holy Spirit to guide us. This isn't a simple three-step process, but it begins with honoring God's way above our own and inviting Him through prayer and study of His words to lead our lives.

I CANNOT PLEASE EVERYONE, BUT I MUST TAKE INTO ACCOUNT THE VIEW OF OTHERS AND CHOOSE EMPATHY.

Honoring God can be difficult not just because of disobedience but also because of distraction. The average person worldwide spends 145 minutes per day on social media. Twenty-four-hour news sells its content by telling us that everything is a crisis, urgent, or needs our attention immediately. Work can now be accessed remotely 24 hours a day, seven days a week. There is so much to do and see. Life can drive our decisions with little reflection if we are not careful. Yet living according to the latest distraction is not how we honor God. I cannot please everyone, but I must take into account the view of others and choose empathy. Intentional living is the opposite of distracted living. And it is a requirement for those who want to honor God consistently in their lives.

HONOR OURSELVES

It may be strange to place honoring yourself before honoring others. I'm not talking about preferring yourself or living selfishly. Instead, honoring consistently starts with believing that you, too, have value to God. I can honor God and others best when I choose to believe what God says about me and to act accordingly.

He starts by telling us who we are. The Bible says that we have been given the power to be children of God. That is what it means to accept Christ's sacrifice and become a Jesus-follower. We become part of God's family. We belong. You are not an outcast or a second-class citizen to God. You are loved, adored, and accepted by your Father in heaven. And you have purpose and value.

The Bible tells us that God created good works in advance for us to do. Not only that, but God promises that the Holy Spirit will empower us to live the life that He has called us to live, loving others, serving them, and bringing heaven to earth through our actions. God says that you are more than a conqueror over the struggles you face, that you can be content in all circumstances, live in joy despite your past, and find peace even when you don't understand. He wraps up all these promises, all these statements about who you are and what you can do by saying that He will personally work everything to the good. So, when we can't see the good, we can trust the providence of God to work even the bad things in our life for the good.

Side note: The Bible doesn't say that everything happens for a reason. That concept is actually from other religions and philosophies. The Bible says in spite of what happens, God is able to work every detail of life for the good of those who love Him. Like an artist with a mosaic, God takes the broken bits and builds something more beautiful than we can imagine.

[D]ON'T DISCOUNT YOUR POTENTIAL TO CONTRIBUTE TO THIS WORLD. YOU WERE BORN WITH PURPOSE.

If you are a child of God on a mission, then it is only fitting that you would honor that mission and yourself by acting accordingly. When you are tempted to slip into self-pity or doubt that you have any value, remember what God has said. Go back to your beliefs. And don't discount your potential to contribute to this world. You were born with purpose.

Here is a practical way to implement honoring yourself in your life. Begin to treat your time and energy as though they were valuable. Go through the exercise of planning your day the night before. Think about what needs to be done, lay out your clothes, prepare your lunch, and then pray that God will show you the good works He has for you along the way. In the morning, get out of bed with purpose. Declare to yourself something like this: "God, this is your day. I believe I am who you say that I am. Help me to see the opportunities to love and honor those around me today." By treating your time and energy as valuable, by acting as though you are on a mission (which you are), you honor yourself and prepare yourself to better honor others.

HONOR OTHERS

James was a half-brother of Jesus. And during Jesus' life, his brothers, including James, were not on board with the mission. We know from the New Testament that Jesus appeared to James after the resurrection. This encounter must have changed everything. James ultimately became a leader in the church and a committed follower of Christ.

The Book of James reflects the heart of a man who found grace when he least deserved it, like all of us if we are honest. Was he thinking of Jesus when he commanded the early church to honor each other consistently? Was he thinking of his own choice not to honor the brother who was too familiar to ever be believed as Savior? Listen to his words:

My brothers and sisters, believers in our glorious Lord Jesus Christ must not show favoritism. Suppose a man comes into your meeting wearing a gold ring and fine clothes, and a poor man in filthy old clothes also comes in. If you show special attention to the man wearing fine clothes and say, "Here's a good seat for you," but say to the poor man, "You stand there" or "Sit on the floor by my feet," have you not discriminated among yourselves and become judges with evil thoughts? (James 2:1–4 NIV).

It's easy to become a judge with evil thoughts. "That person deserves their situation." "If I were them, I would. . ." And it is natural to prefer the easy person, the wealthy person, the person who can do more for me, the person who looks like me. James tells us to reject the easy way and go with the Jesus way. He doesn't say it is natural or better for you. He doesn't say it will lead to a happier or wealthier or more fulfilling life. Instead, James says if I believe in our glorious Lord Jesus Christ, I cannot, must not discriminate. I must honor consistently.

Roman society was based on hierarchies of class and ethnicity. Your class, your ethnicity, your gender, your birth determined how you were treated, what rights you held, who you could become, and how you were honored when you walked into a room. What James was writing to the churches in this passage was countercultural and even subversive. And it still is today.

In the late 1980s, Pastor Denny Duron was confronted with a choice—embrace discrimination and make "everyone" happy or follow Jesus and stir up trouble. The private school his mother founded wanted to offer varsity sports. So they applied to join a small private-school league. The meeting with the league officials went great until they asked what percentage of minorities the school would welcome, helpfully suggesting 10 percent. Pastor Denny had a temper. And this question set him off. He quickly responded, "One hundred percent, hopefully." They didn't hear from the league again and were not invited to join. Instead, they turned to the public-school league, where they had no small amount of success.

These types of stories are infuriating, especially when we understand Christians are involved on both sides. They are much too common. Now, perhaps the question would not be so boldly stated. Perhaps now, the prejudice that destroys our society would be cloaked in code language. We would be fools to think that prejudice, racism, sexism, classism, favoritism do not exist both in our world and in our own hearts. And we can hear James pleading with us from two-thousand years ago, "My brothers and sisters, believers in our glorious Lord Jesus Christ must not show favoritism" (James 2:1 NIV).

[W]E SHOULD HONOR EVERYONE THAT WE COME INTO CONTACT WITH.

Honor should not be some strange set of customs surrounding leadership or those in authority. Instead, we should honor everyone that we come into contact with. We honor *consistently*. Another way to say this might be that we serve everyone around us with the same heart and attitude.

The word "honor" evokes memories of the round table, gentlemanly duels, and maybe Camelot. Biblically, God requires that we show honor to Him, those in authority, our parents, and those to whom honor is due (Proverbs 3:9; Romans 13:1–7; Exodus 20:12; 1 Peter 3:15). Jesus makes it clear that we are required to go beyond the enumerated and even logical recipients of honor to serve everyone around us (Mark 9:35).

MOST WHO HAVE TROUBLE WITH HONOR, OR SERVING, ALSO HAVE TROUBLE WITH HUMILITY.

We honor others because we choose to be honorable. Honorable simply means "characterized by integrity: guided by a keen sense of duty and ethical conduct."[18] In other words, the way we treat people doesn't flow out of our evaluation of their "worthiness" but an identity of humble submission to God's commands. Our actions are guided by our sense of duty to God's words and His love for us. The Bible tells us that honor requires humility (Proverbs 15:33). In fact, humility is the posture we are to take toward each other in every way and in every circumstance (1 Peter 5:5). Most who have trouble with honor, or serving, also have trouble with humility.

Humbly obeying God should result in our honoring and serving each other consistently. God most often calls out sins that we would easily pass over. These are sins of dishonor, sins such as injustice, unfairness, unwillingness to help family, failure to help the poor, and failure to generally give honor and add value to all those around us. God makes sure that we know He disapproves of gossiping and stirring up trouble and saying cruel words. He takes it seriously when we use our mouths to praise Him one moment and curse our neighbor the next.

WE HONOR THROUGH SERVING

YOU HAVE BEEN GIVEN A SPECIAL GRACE,
A GIFT, WITH WHICH TO HUMBLY SERVE
AND HONOR THOSE AROUND YOU.

God places a value on His people, especially the most vulnerable. He is concerned with how we treat each other. "You, my brothers and sisters, were called to be free. But do not use your freedom to indulge the flesh; rather, serve one another humbly in love" (Galatians 5:13 NIV). God has called us to be free and use that freedom not to serve ourselves but others. Being honorable requires humility, and humility comes from a true understanding of grace. When we truly understand the grace that God has given us, it should compel us to use that grace to serve each other. Jesus is the personification of grace. And yet, grace also includes those gifts Christ has given us to serve each other (1 Peter 4:10). You have been given a special grace, a gift, with which to humbly serve and honor those around you.

Pastor Clarrissa Stephens, the Connection Pastor at NCC, is graced with the gift of hospitality. She does more than make a room pretty; she creates an inviting atmosphere where everyone feels welcomed. And she can do this anywhere. It doesn't matter if it is in a classroom or in her own home. Somehow, when Clarrissa is in charge, you feel like you belong from the moment you walk in the door. It's a gift that she uses to serve others consistently. The people you find at her gatherings are diverse in every sense of the word. She has embraced the Jesus mandate, spoken by James: don't play favorites.

WHEN WE HONOR CONSISTENTLY, WE ARE
CHOOSING TO VALUE GOD'S WORDS OVER
OUR CULTURE AND OUR EMOTIONS.

What is your grace gift? Do not take this as a super spiritual or super metaphysical question. It is practical. What are you good at doing? How have you trained yourself to add value to the world around you? Are you great with numbers, fascinated by athletics, an accomplished pianist? We all have grace gifts. And we are all called to use those gifts to serve the world! When we serve, we are truly honoring in the Biblical sense. When we honor consistently, we are choosing to value God's words over our culture and our emotions.

WE HONOR WITH OUR WORDS

HONOR IS SPEAKING TO OTHERS AND ABOUT OTHERS IN A WAY THAT REINFORCES GOD'S VIEW OF THEM AND GOD'S LOVE FOR THEM.

One way we can all honor consistently is through our words. Let me be clear: honor is not flattery. It isn't lying or saying someone is good at something or the best when he clearly is not in the least. We have another habit, "Practicing Honesty," that comes into play to bring balance here. Honor is speaking to others and about others in a way that reinforces God's view of them and God's love for them.

All the promises of God for your life are true for your neighbor as well. Sometimes, we forget that if God loves and values us because we are part of the world He died for, every person we pass is also loved and valued. Do they know? Do they see the value that God has placed on them? So often, we are quick to judge rather than to honor. If a princess walked into your home believing that she was a pauper, wouldn't you point out her true identity rather than chastise her for wearing clothes that didn't fit her rank? When we speak life and truth to others, when we tell them how God adores them and values them, we honor who they are in the most truthful of ways. God sees me. God loves me. God came to rescue me. And the same is true for you, too.

Destiny's mom, DeAnza Duron, is a believer in creating moments of intentional honor. At every birthday, anniversary, and family gathering, she takes a moment and makes sure we have a chance to be honored and to honor others. She calls it the Circle of Honor. We've adopted the practice into our home, our church, and even our groups. I've seen a similar practice in many homes and communities around the world. There is something powerful about using our words intentionally to honor and bring life to those around us.

The Bible tells us that there is power to create and destroy, bring life and death in our mouths. When we use our words to honor, we bring life and remind another person they are valuable. Oftentimes, we do not speak up because we feel embarrassed, assume they already know, or worry about what they will think of us. Do not allow fear or assumption to rob you and those around you of hearing words that bring life. My family did not grow up with words of honor; at first, we were not interested in saying kind things to each other in any formal setting. We preferred to joke and tease. That's good too, but something beautiful happened when we began to honor each other with our words. It's one thing to believe your family is proud; it is another to hear it.

One of our groups at NCC implemented intentional words of honor for each birthday. A woman who had attended just a short time was left in tears as her group began to speak about the strength they saw in her, the joy she added to the room, and how they were confident that the best was yet to come in her life. She later told her leader that no one had ever spoken to her like that before. It was the beginning of a life transformation. And all it took was a few moments of intentional honor and a room of brave women willing to speak life, hope, and love.

There are people in your life who are waiting for you to use your words to show them where they are valuable. Your co-worker needs to know you think he is great at his job. Your sister wants to hear how you admire her even now that you are grown. Your teacher needs to see the ways she's impacted your life. Too often, we leave the words of honor until the funeral. I encourage you to choose to honor consistently, speak up regularly, and bring life to those around you through your words.

WE ARE EMPOWERED BY THE HOLY SPIRIT TO HONOR

///

EVERYONE IS DESERVING OF HONOR, AND EVERYONE
IS SOMEONE GOD HAS ASKED ME TO SERVE.

\\

When we are committed to honoring and serving consistently, it changes the way we think and respond. No longer are there groups of people it is okay to "go off" on. Everyone is deserving of honor, and everyone is someone God has asked me to serve. Thankfully, the Holy Spirit produces fruit in us that is beyond our natural ability. Self-control is one of the fruits of the Spirit—the result of living a Christ-centered life. It takes self-control to honor consistently in a world where many act dishonorably. We choose, empowered by the Holy Spirit, to honor consistently, not occasionally.

The apostle Paul said it this way: "Love one another with brotherly affection. Outdo one another in showing honor" (Romans 12:10 ESV). He further explained, "Never pay back evil with more evil. Do things in such a way that everyone can see you are honorable" (Romans 12:17 NLT). How would my life change if I determined to apply this principle to every situation? What would your life look like if you did the same? Can you imagine a world where we spent our time thinking of how to honor and serve rather than pay back evil? This is the freedom that consistently honoring offers.

As a community, we have determined to wrap our relationships in the bubble wrap of honor consistently. We choose to serve each other. After all, Christ served us. How can we honor those who are seemingly undeserving? Very practically, we honor the principle. If God says to honor and serve, we simply choose to obey Him. We do not ask whether someone is deserving but rather whether God is deserving of our obedience.

Say it Again:

- Honor reflects what we value in life.
- As Christians, honoring requires us to choose to value what God values over our own preferences.
- We honor God through our obedience.
- We honor ourselves by choosing to believe that we have value and treating ourselves with respect as created beings loved by God.
- We honor others consistently by choosing to see everyone as valuable to God and, therefore, valuable to us.
- We can honor through serving and using our grace gifts to add value to those around us.
- We can honor through intentional words of encouragement.
- As Christians, we are empowered by the Holy Spirit to honor consistently.

Make it Personal:

- What does it mean to honor others?
- What grace gifts has God given you to serve the community with?
- How can you practically bring honor to those closest to you through your words?
- Right now, write down the names of three people that you want to intentionally honor with your words. Hold yourself accountable by giving yourself a due date.
- Where can you see favoritism creeping into your attitudes and actions? Repent and ask God to allow you to love others the way He loves them.
- Decide that honor is not about others but about obedience to Christ.

WE LEAN IN

A good stance and posture reflect a proper state of mind.
—Morihei Ueshiba

*Choosing to be positive and having a grateful attitude is
going to determine how you're going to live your life.*
—Joel Osteen

*Whatever you do, work at it with all your heart, as working for the Lord,
not for human masters, since you know that you will receive an inheritance
from the Lord as a reward. It is the Lord Christ you are serving.*
(Colossians 3:23 NIV)

Athletes are fanatical about form. Form can make the difference in a race, a game, or even in a workout session. Form matters. Leaning in speaks to our form, our posture. And as a House Habit, "We Lean In" is our chosen posture of mind, heart, and body.

YOUR PHYSICAL POSTURE MATTERS

In terms of health, bad posture causes back pain and contributes to poor circulation. Good posture engages your core, opens up your diaphragm, and aids in digestion. Bad physical posture can cause you to feel sluggish and even fearful. Good physical posture increases energy, productivity, and reduces stress levels.[19] In terms of communication, bad physical posture whispers to your audience that you might be nervous, unprepared, or indifferent, regardless of the internal truth. On the other hand, good posture communicates to your audience that you are ready, prepared, in control, and confident.[20] Posture matters.

Our physical posture is critical in part because it can direct our emotional and mental posture. It is also the easiest to notice and change. At NCC, we engage our physical posture intentionally during sermons, in conversations, and when we have fun together. We physically choose to lean in because we don't want to sit back. We are not passive. We are not critics and cynics. We are not skeptical or apathetic. We are ready to take action. Our posture says, "I'm ready. I'm excited. I'm engaged. I'm with you. Let's do this!"

YOU CONTROL YOUR LEAN

Bad day? Tough weekend? Difficult season? You can choose to lean in anyway. Chances are, the harder you lean in, the faster you will get through whatever you are going through.

Leaning in is counter-cultural because we live in a lean-back society. We lean back and judge. We lean back and avoid responsibility. We take time to criticize the White House, but our own house is in chaos. We have the solutions for everyone else's problems, but our own lives are dysfunctional. Our culture leans back and blames anyone, everyone, all the humans except for this one. You will fit in if you lean back. Everyone is doing it. Leaning back makes you the judge, and it can cause you to feel powerful, even though you are not.

WE LEAN IN BECAUSE IT IS WORTH THE RISK OF FAILURE TO HAVE THE CHANCE TO TASTE SUCCESS.

We lean in because we cannot control "them," but we can control ourselves. We lean in and take responsibility for our own chaos instead of judging others. We lean in because it is worth the risk of failure to have the chance to taste success. We lean in because we only have one life and one moment, and we do not want to waste it. Leaning in happens when we tire of *feeling* powerful and yearn to actually become powerful.

The apostle Paul said, "So I run with purpose in every step. I am not just shadowboxing" (1 Corinthians 9:26 NLT). That is vivid imagery. Paul was leaning in to the fight. You can't fight your best fight leaning back. You have to lean in. He goes on to say, "I discipline my body like an athlete, training it to do what it should" (1 Corinthians 9:27 NLT). Paul knew that if I don't force myself to lean in, I will naturally lean back. I have to discipline myself to develop the habit of leaning in, to develop the habit of taking responsibility, to develop the habit of listening with intention. Why? Because leaning back is comfortable, but leaning in demands something from me.

Leaning in is a posture that puts me in a position to WIN! Paul starts off this whole passage of scripture by saying, "run to win" (1 Corinthians 9:24 NLT). We can't win if we don't lean in! If I posture myself correctly, I can position myself effectively!

YOUR LEAN DETERMINES YOUR DIRECTION

Growing up in the south, riding a bike is the ultimate freedom for a ten-year-old. The bounds of where you can go and what you can do expand exponentially. There is nothing like riding with the wind whipping around you on a hot summer day toward your friends and all of the adventures of the day. I used to love riding as fast as I could and then leaning into the turns even to go faster. One thing about bike riding is you pay for distraction. If you start looking away from your destination too long and hard, you will inevitably steer off course. Why? Your attention affects your lean, and your lean will determine your direction.

Try the same concept when you are walking. Walking is little more than organized falling, it has been said, and it is true. We lean a direction, take a literal step of faith, and repeat over and over again until we reach our destination. You can't walk well one way while leaning another. Your lean determines your direction.

YOUR LEAN DETERMINES YOUR DIRECTION.

In life, it is the same. What I lean into will determine my direction. As a college student, if you lean into the history department, go to lectures, talk with professors, taking extra classes, you are more likely to end up with a history minor or major. Your lean determines your direction. If you lean into your marriage, cultivating it with classes and counseling, thinking positive thoughts about your spouse, trying to give 100%, you will likely begin to move toward a better marriage. Your lean determines your direction.

A few years ago, Destiny decided to go in a different direction in her career. She is a trained lawyer but had been working as a supply chain consultant for a decade. After years of wishing she was still working in the legal field, she took action and started leaning into relationships, opportunities, and mentors who would take her life in the direction she wanted to go. Within a few months, she was practicing law for clients she enjoyed and moving towards a thriving practice.

WE LEAN IN LIFE BY THE WAY THAT WE SPEND OUR TIME, ATTENTION, AND EMOTIONAL ENERGY.

What changed Destiny's life? It was a choice to lean differently. We lean in life by the way that we spend our time, attention, and emotional energy. We lean with what we choose to embrace. If I want to go in a different direction in life, I will have to begin leaning a different way. Destiny had spent years leaning into the emotions of wishing things were different. This didn't change her direction. It was only when she began leaning into change instead of regret that life took a different turn.

I have heard people say that Christianity just didn't "work" for them. They went to church for years, and it never "clicked." That is a lot like leaning back and trying to walk forward. If I want a relationship with Christ, I must lean in that direction. I must spend my time, attention, and emotional energy cultivating a community that will support my faith, reading the Bible, praying. I cannot just wish my way into a different faith position. I have to take action. I have to lean differently to live differently.

Don't be overwhelmed with all the different things that you *need* to lean into or the different directions you can go. We can't change everything overnight. Just think of one thing you are leaning into that is sending your life on a negative path and stop that one thing, or even begin doing it less. Then think of one thing you could lean into that would start moving you toward the life you want to live and begin doing that thing more. Baby steps matter.

Most importantly, examine your life direction! Today, write down where you would like to be next year and ask yourself whether what you are leaning into today will get you there. If your lean determines your direction, your direction can also help you see where to adjust your lean. Maybe you will need a coach or mentor or friend to help you along the way. Just remember that the life you want to live, a life of mission, will require the habit, not the one-time event of leaning in. So, resolve to keep practicing and adjusting regularly.

YOUR LEAN EXPOSES YOUR ATTITUDE

OUR ATTITUDE AFFECTS OUR LEAN, BUT OUR LEAN CAN BE ADJUSTED TO CHANGE OUR ATTITUDE.

Attitude isn't just the way that your teenager responds when asked to clean his room. As we stated earlier, attitude is your settled way of thinking or feeling about someone or something. And like your teenager's response, it shows up even when we are trying to hide it. Our attitude affects our lean, but our lean can be adjusted to change our attitude. Here is an example. You may be walking around slump-shouldered. You feel a little tired, maybe even a little depressed. There is some pain in your back. Suddenly, something reminds you to stand up straight! You stand up, and your posture impacts your attitude. You are breathing in more oxygen; your spine is more aligned. Your physiology is affecting your psychology. In other words, your attitude has changed because your lean has changed.

Oftentimes, we come into situations with a particular lean that comes from our settled way of thinking or feeling about the situation, our attitude. The conversation with our mother-in-law has not even started, but we are already bored. We aren't going to lean in to what she has to say, because our settled way of thinking of her is, "She is so boring!" Our lean is exposing our attitude. The fight with our spouse hasn't even begun, but we are already on the way out the door mentally. We aren't going to lean in and try to resolve things or love big because our settled way of thinking about conflict is, "Not worth it!" Our lean is exposing our attitude. The sermon hasn't yet begun, but we are getting comfy for our short morning nap. Okay, maybe that one is too personal!

If we want to change our attitude, we can start with our beliefs, but we can also observe our attitude from our lean and use our lean to change our attitude. This is sometimes called environmental shaping. When Destiny went to college, her Dean encouraged her to lean into class not by adopting a certain attitude but by sitting in the front. Why? He knew that her lean could shape her way of thinking and feeling about the class.

Sitting in the back with your hat pulled down low and cowboy boots propped up sends a signal not just to everyone else about your attitude, but it tells you how to feel as well. Your body is reinforcing your mind's decision not to take this moment seriously or value this opportunity. Choosing to sit in the front is an easy first step to confronting and changing your attitude. Your lean is exposing your attitude, but it can also be the catalyst to changing your attitude.

> HE ASKED HIS DISCIPLES TO FOLLOW HIM
> BEFORE HE EVER ASKED THEM TO CHANGE THEIR
> ATTITUDES OR BELIEFS OR EVEN HABITS.

Think about the way that Jesus operated. He asked His disciples to follow Him before He ever asked them to change their attitudes or beliefs or even habits. He knew that if we will take action to lean in, we will put ourselves in a better posture to progress in our lives. What small steps can you take that will cause you to lean in before you ever feel like leaning in? Here are some ideas!

Marriage: Schedule a date night and really listen to your spouse. Ask new questions—there are lists all over the internet. Join a marriage small group at your church. Make an appointment with a counselor.

Work: Arrive earlier than usual. Dress with excellence. Change your lunch table to sit around people who have the position you want. Choose to answer every request with energy rather than passivity.

Parenting: Put your phone in your bedroom for a couple of hours in the evening. Choose a book and read it to your kids. Let them pick a game and play it with them.

Friendship: Make a monthly date with your friends and keep it! Let each person pick a new experience that everyone will try.

These are all areas where our attitude can get stuck and take our lean with it. We can find ourselves leaning out when we need to lean in to go forward. When your lean exposes your attitude, don't despair. Use your lean to adjust your attitude and move you closer to the life you've always wanted to live!

MISSION REQUIRES US TO LEAN IN

Leaning in works as a habit in every area of life. However, these House Habits exist in the midst of the mission we talked about in the first few chapters. We are leaning in so that we can create Christ-centered, culture-changing community. So, here are a few things that a mission-minded Christ-follower will need to lean into on a regular basis.

LEAN IN TO CHRIST

As Christ-followers, we must first lean into Christ every day. Jesus often said things that were difficult for His disciples to understand. Sometimes, what He said was offensive or almost impossible to accept. One day, Jesus said what must have seemed like blasphemy to a people who were expressly forbidden to eat the blood of animals, much less humans. "I tell you the truth, unless you eat the flesh of the Son of Man and drink his blood, you cannot have eternal life within you. But anyone who eats my flesh and drinks my blood has eternal life, and I will raise that person at the last day. For my flesh is true food, and my blood is true drink" (John 6:53–55 NLT).

Not surprisingly, many of Jesus' disciples left Him. It was just too much. Drink blood? Who does this guy think He is? Jesus turned to His closest followers, the twelve disciples He had hand chosen, and asked, "Are you also going to leave?" (John 6:67 NLT). Can you imagine how they felt at that moment? The apostle Peter is my favorite disciple because he just says things the way he sees them. Peter does not sugarcoat his perspective, even when perhaps he should. "Simon Peter replied, 'Lord, to whom would we go? You have the words that give eternal life. We believe, and we know you are the Holy One of God'" (John 6:68–69 NLT). Peter wasn't saying following Jesus was easy. He wasn't saying, "Oh yes, Jesus. I'm completely comfortable with the cannibalism teaching you just threw out there." Peter wasn't even saying he understood the message behind the words. Peter just said the truth. If I don't lean into you, there is nothing else to lean into.

Sometimes life will be confusing. Sometimes we will not understand the season we are in. Sometimes we will encounter disappointment, disillusionment, and disagreements that try to strip us of our courage to lean in. If Christ is not the core of our lives, if He is not the one we lean into the most, if the gospel is not the foundation on which we stand, then no other lean will really matter. We have to learn to lean into Christ every single day.

LEAN IN TO COMMUNITY

Want to become a better athlete? Lose weight? Complete that exercise circuit? Studies say you should join a group. As we've already discussed, people who exercise in groups are more likely to stick with it, push themselves harder, and as a result have better results on average than those who go it alone. Leaning into a healthy lifestyle is easier when you lean into community.[21] It doesn't matter if it is CrossFit or Camp Gladiator or a neighborhood aerobics class. What matters is the community!

> DON'T ALLOW CHURCH TO BE THE PLACE
> WHERE YOU ARE LEAST LIKE YOURSELF.

Just like working out is easier in groups, living a Christ-focused life is easier in community (Hebrews 10:25 NLT). Every week, around the world, there are hundreds of thousands of communities of believers leaning in to Christ together. They have learned that leaning in to the Bible, worship, and prayer is easier when you lean into community at the same time. Sometimes, we run from community because we are intimidated or embarrassed. We assume everyone else has it together. And we think we are the only ones in need of a posture reset on a daily, sometimes hourly, basis. It's just not true. We all need community. Don't allow church to be the place where you are least like yourself. Be vulnerable, let people get close, and lean in together.

LEAN IN TO WORSHIP

When we are in a corporate setting, we have a chance to lean in to the presence of God together. Our posture matters when we sing and when we praise together. There is always an inward struggle to focus when we come together. There are the bad choices of the week, the familial pressures, the tasks to be done, the disappointments, the hurts, the doubts that weigh on our minds and can change our posture from lean in to lean back. When we choose to lean in during the singing, whether we feel like it or not, we are choosing to physically move beyond our emotions and open ourselves to what God would do in us today. We move from the past into the present simply by changing our posture.

Our particular Christian expression encourages singing loudly, lifting hands, even swaying and clapping (Psalm 134:2). Maybe your church is quieter. Regardless, be engaged during the singing parts of the service. Lean in to God's presence. Lean past your emotions. Lean past your inward struggles. Often I do not feel like lifting my hands when I walk into church, but I have made a habit of leaning in to God's presence. So, I lift my hands in surrender. I sing the words on the screen as a declaration of faith. I close my eyes to shut out distraction. And before long, my emotions have come into alignment with my physical posture and I have connected with God's presence.

Sometimes, it is more beneficial to act your way into a feeling than to feel your way into an action. Feeling your way into an action may result in a lifetime of inaction. If I wait to act in a loving way toward my spouse, I am leaving our relationship subject to the whims of emotion. If I instead choose to act in a loving way, despite my feelings, I will often find my feelings following my actions. When I choose to glorify God with my whole heart, with my hands, with my voice, regardless of my feelings, I, in the same way, am acknowledging that my relationship with Him goes deeper than the emotional.

David understood this. He intentionally leaned in to God's presence. "Praise the Lord, my soul; all my inmost being, praise his holy name" (Psalm 103:1 NIV). David is commanding himself to praise God. He is putting a demand on his own nature to submit and lean in to God's presence.

The chapter goes on to tell us how David would motivate himself to lean in. He recounted God's goodness and declared God's faithfulness.

*Praise the Lord, my soul, and forget not all his benefits—who forgives
all your sins and heals all your diseases, who redeems your life from
the pit and crowns you with love and compassion, who satisfies your
desires with good things so that your youth is renewed like the eagle's.*
(PSALM 103:2-5 NIV)

IN HIS PRESENCE IS PEACE, JOY, POWER, GRACE, MERCY, LOVE, BREAKTHROUGH, HEALING, AND SO MUCH MORE.

When we choose to change our posture, when we choose to lean in to God's presence by intentionally engaging in the moment, lifting our hands, declaring God's goodness, reminding ourselves of His faithfulness, we open ourselves to the changing power found only in His presence. In His presence is peace, joy, power, grace, mercy, love, breakthrough, healing, and so much more. I may not feel it, but I don't want to miss what God has for me!

We do not have to be in church to lean in to the presence of God, but church is a great place to practice. I can lean in to God's presence early in the morning in my home by intentionally turning on worship music, singing a hymn, declaring God's goodness. I can lean in to God's presence as I drive to work by turning off the radio and reminding myself out loud of how faithful He has been to me and my family. I can lean in to God's presence on my lunch break, while the kids nap, during family devotions at night, even as I go to sleep. I simply need to change my posture from waiting for God to move my emotions to choosing to intentionally lean in to His presence.

LEAN IN TO THE BIBLE

Not only do we have a chance to practice leaning in to God's presence when we come together as a church, but we also can practice leaning in to His words. The scriptures are alive with hope and change and power. When we come together to hear God's words through preaching or spoken word or drama, we have the chance to practice leaning in. Every Sunday at NCC, we have a declaration we say together before the preaching begins. This is really our lean in reminder. The end of the declaration goes like this: "Holy Spirit, open up my eyes to see, my ears to hear, my mind to understand, and my heart to receive everything that God has for me today." Wow! God has something for me today! And that is true every single day of the year.

WHEN YOU ARE LISTENING, YOU ARE ACTUALLY PREPARING TO FEED YOURSELF.

When I choose to lean in to the teaching of God's word, I am heeding the words of Proverbs. "Listen to advice and accept instruction, that you may gain wisdom in the future" (Proverbs 19:20 ESV). Listening is not passive; it is active! When you are listening, you are actually preparing to feed yourself. When we listen with intention to receive, we store up truth we can take away and grow from all throughout the week.

I do not just mean we should metaphorically lean in to the teaching. I encourage you to actually change your posture. Physically lean in as you listen. Take notes. Try saying, "Amen." Changing your response, changing your posture creates an anticipation for what is about to take place. Your posture says to yourself, the speaker, and your neighbor, "I'm fully expecting something supernatural to take place." There is truth in the words of God, and I want to fully lean in to that truth.

We do not have to be in a group to lean in to the Bible. At home, we can listen to the Bible, read the Bible, and do studies about the Bible on our own. The important thing is to lean in to those moments. Don't just read the verse of the day casually. Say it out loud, read it in context, take a moment and think of how it could apply to your life today. Leaning in to the Bible looks like being intentional with our reading and study, even on our own.

LEAN IN TO THE FUTURE

Amen literally means "So be it." It is a way of agreeing with what has been said. We say Amen at the end of prayers. We say Amen at the end of sentences that we feel strongly about. We say Amen when we want to indicate that we, too, are in alignment with the speaker's words. It is a verbal way of leaning in.

MY POSTURE IS MY EXPECTATION DECLARATION.

Leaning in puts us in agreement with what God says. The truth never impacts our lives until we get into agreement with the truth. That is why we should not be afraid to say, "Amen!" It is easier to say Amen when I have already postured myself, prepared myself to receive. My posture is my expectation declaration. I am leaning in because I expect to receive something from what is being taught. Moreover, I expect to receive something from God. It is hard for me to receive the greatness of God's declarations when I have low expectations!

And as Christ-followers, should we not have great expectations? Greater is He that is in me than He that is in the world (1 John 4:4). No weapon formed against me can prosper (Isaiah 54:17). Nothing can separate me from the love of God (Romans 8:38). I am His child (1 John 3). He is the creator of the world (Genesis 1:1). He has already overcome death, hell, and the grave (Revelation 1:18). And He loves me! (Romans 5:8). Why shouldn't I walk into every church service or Bible study with the expectation that He has something special for me to receive?

One of my favorite Bible miracles is the woman who leaned in. Maybe you are unfamiliar with that title, but I think the story will be familiar. Luke records that as Jesus was traveling, He passed a woman who had been hemorrhaging for twelve years. She pressed through the crowd, and then she leaned in toward Jesus and was instantly healed. She did not have faith that Jesus would stop. She did not have faith that He would choose her to heal out of the crowd, but she had faith that if she leaned in enough, she could touch the hem of His garment and that would be all she would need to be healed (Luke 8:43–48). Leaning in does not take a lot of faith. It just takes a little faith. It takes the next step. And God will use that little faith to heal our souls and change our lives. Change your posture. Change your life. Lean in.

I'm grateful for those who have leaned in for me when I could not lean in for myself.

In the corporate setting, your lean can help those around you. Luke also describes a miracle of four men who gave their lean to their friend. These were four friends who carried their crippled friend to Jesus. They tore the roof off a house. They lowered their friend through the roof. And Jesus healed him. The crippled man was unable to lean in to Jesus for himself. He was unable to move. His friends let him borrow their lean (Luke 5:17–39). When you lean in to God's words for others, it can make all the difference. Sometimes it is as simple as saying Amen to keep your neighbor engaged. Sometimes it is picking up a friend for church so he has no excuse. Sometimes it is writing verses on a card and taping them to a depressed friend's mirror. I'm grateful for those who have leaned in for me when I could not lean in for myself.

When we lean in to Christ, into God's presence and the truth of God's word, it puts us in a position to love those around us. Loving people isn't easy. Yet that is what we are all called to do. We are called to lean in. We lean in to Christ so that we can love the world. That is exactly what Jesus did for us. God leaned into the world because we needed a Savior. And we are called to love the world the way Jesus loved us. We are called to lean in.

LEAN IN TO CHALLENGES

We must also lean in to the challenges around us. Jesus was constantly teaching His disciples to lean in to the difficulties around them. Once, when Jesus was teaching in the wilderness, His disciples brought to His attention that the people were hungry and should be sent away so they could eat. I'm sure they were proud of their proactive observation! And yet Jesus replied with a very distinct, "Lean in!" He said, "You give them something to eat." What? Jesus was reminding them that the problems of this world are not the responsibility of someone else (Matthew 14). We know the answer, and we have to lean in to the challenges around us.

Early in our time at NCC, we were given the choice to lean in or lean back from a problem in our community. In our parish—that is the Louisiana word for county in case you are confused—all students are required to wear uniforms. One day, as Destiny was trying to finish up some work at the church, a very distraught woman walked into our foyer. The woman proceeded to say that she had asked every church on our street for help and that no one would help her. This was not a good sign. Usually if other churches won't help you, we can't help you either. She was trying to find a church in our area, in her words, to simply collect uniforms for students who could not afford to buy them. Just collect them, she said. We will do the rest. Who could say no? Also, we didn't have very many other things planned because we had little to no budget and were just getting started. So, we began collecting the uniforms and investigating the need. It turns out that our area has a high number of children in poverty. We were happy to help collect uniforms. What an easy win. After all, we lean in, right? Then, the other shoe dropped, and we realized why all the older and wiser churches had said no.

WHEN WE ALL LEAN IN TOGETHER, PROBLEMS TEND TO BECOME MUCH SMALLER AND EASIER TO MANAGE.

There was no real plan to distribute the uniforms. Our team went from collecting uniforms to becoming the hub for distributing hundreds of uniforms to hundreds of families in a day to providing needed uniforms directly to schools. It would have been easy to give up, lean back, remind God that our location only had one paid staffer at the time. It would have been easy to look to other organizations with bigger budgets and more resources. But we leaned in to the problem, not because we felt like it but because we have a habit. Since that time, we have given away over 18,000 uniforms in ten years and reached thousands of families in our community. The Back-to-School uniform giveaway is the highlight of our church calendar. Now other organizations are beginning to join in and hold their own uniform giveaways. This is exactly what we hope and pray for every time we lean in to a gap. After all, when we all lean in together, problems tend to become much smaller and easier to manage.

We include this story not to pat our community on the back. No. It is a reminder that when we lean in to the challenges around us, God will meet us in the midst of the challenge. I could tell you story after story of divine appointments and miraculous provision. One year, we had more families arrive than uniforms. Somehow, we were able to give something to everyone. My staff was convinced the uniforms had multiplied. I was convinced they miscounted. Regardless, God met us in the moment and met the needs of those around us because we chose to step over fear and lean in. Next time you see a challenge in your community, remember the words of Jesus: "You give them something to eat." And choose to lean in.

WHAT KEEPS US FROM LEANING IN?

Leaning in does not look like leaning on a crutch. There is a big difference between a runner leaning toward the finish line and a man leaning on a walking stick. And there is a temptation to trade your lean in for a lean on in life. Proverbs understood this tension. "Trust in the Lord with all your heart, and do not lean on your own understanding. In all your ways acknowledge him, and he will make straight your paths" (Proverbs 3:5–6 ESV). This verse sums up the struggle—lean in to the Lord or lean on our own ways. It is a difficult choice and one we must make every single day.

There are four things we often lean on that will keep us from leaning in:

1) **Losses**. We can't lean on our losses if we want to lean in to what God has for us. In athletics, teams lose their next game because they haven't stopped thinking about their last game. When you stay focused on a loss, the chances are higher that you will lose again. There is a reason people talk about a losing streak in athletics. In life, if you continue to lean on your losses to make decisions, choose friendships, and protect your emotions, you will lose again and again.

Leaning on losses means we put the emphasis on the wrong thing. Everyone loses, but you don't have to feel like a loser. Everyone has been defeated from time to time, but you don't have to stay defeated. When we lose, we have a choice: will I lean on or learn from my loss? The enemy always wants you to lean on your loss, stay there, don't move on. God wants you to learn the lesson from your loss so you can effectively lean in to Him and the future He has for you! Our losses should not keep us from leaning in. Rather, they should encourage us to lean in harder! When we lose, we need more of God, more of the community, more encouragement than we did before.

LEANING ON OUR EMOTIONS LEADS TO US DESIRING SENSATIONS WHEN WE NEED A GOOD FOUNDATION.

2) **Emotions**. We cannot lean on our emotions. Proverbs again has the answer. "A sound mind makes for a robust body, but runaway emotions corrode the bones" (Proverbs 14:30 MSG). Runaway emotions remind me of an amusement park ride that jerks you

up and down and all around. It is fun for a moment, but it is a terrible way to live life. Leaning on our emotions leads to us desiring sensations when we need a good foundation. When I need a sensation, I go seeking the wrong things to fill my need. I'm leaning on my emotions to get me through rather than leaning in to God to change me from the inside out.

We often see church people who have spiritualized their lean on emotions. They are constantly church shopping, looking for a better experience. They will look for a new word from God, even when they haven't obeyed the last one. They are constantly finding new "prayer partners" who will listen to them, comfort them, affirm them, but never challenge them. Don't spiritualize your emotional crutches. Instead, throw them to the side and lean in to a God that provides a firm foundation!

Jesus told us in Matthew, "Seek the Kingdom of God above all else, and live righteously, and he will give you everything you need" (Matthew 6:33 NLT). In other words, don't look for validation or false emotional support from those around you; spend your time seeking God's kingdom and He will give you everything you need. Your feelings should not be used to judge your faith. Instead, your faith should stand as the judge of your feelings. There is nothing wrong with having emotions, even lots of emotions. The problem is when our emotions attempt to trump our devotion to God. Leaning in demands devotion. Don't get stuck leaning on your emotions.

3) **Old approaches**. It is so easy to lean on an old approach to life. After all, what got me here was pretty good! One of the saddest phrases I hear is, "That's just the way I am." Another I have banished from our church, home, and business is, "That's the way it's always been done." There is nothing sacred about what has always been done. In fact, our old ways can begin to obstruct our future.

DON'T ALLOW AN OLD APPROACH TO HOLD YOU BACK FROM FULLY LEANING IN TO THE WILL AND PURPOSE OF GOD IN YOUR LIFE.

Paul counsels against leaning on old approaches. "You were taught, with regard to your former way of life, to put off your old self, which is being corrupted by its deceitful desires; to be made new in the attitude of your minds; and to put on the new self, created to be like God in true righteousness and holiness" (Ephesians 4:22–24 NIV). We are new in our attitudes. We have a new self. And we have to constantly throw off the old self. Sometimes, those who grew up in the church think falsely that this only applies to those outside church walls. Not so! Jesus was brutal to those in the religious community who held on to old approaches at the expense of the community around them. Don't allow an old approach to hold you back from fully leaning in to the will and purpose of God in your life.

DON'T LEAN ON NORMAL. LEAN IN TO THE SUPERNATURAL.

4) **Normal.** If you are leaning on normal, then it will be impossible for you to lean in to the supernatural power of God. Paul tried in his letters to explain to us and the early church just how incredibly powerful God truly is. "I also pray that you will understand the incredible greatness of God's power for us who believe him. This is the same mighty power that raised Christ from the dead and seated him in the place of honor at God's right hand in the heavenly realms" (Ephesians 1:19–20 NLT). This is not normal. Jesus didn't die for normal. He didn't defeat death, hell, and the grave for normal. He didn't break the power of sin for normal.

He offers us the supernatural in exchange for our normal. Don't lean on normal. Lean in to the supernatural.

WARNING: LEANING IN WILL CHANGE YOUR LIFE

I do have to warn you. Leaning in will change your life. It will change the way you worship. It will change the way you listen in church. It will change the way you read your Bible. It will change the way you pray. It will change the way you love those around you. It will change the way you see the challenges in your community. Leaning in will change your life. And that is exactly why you should do it.

> LEANING IN REQUIRES US TO CHANGE OUR POSTURE, GIVE UP OUR CRUTCHES, AND ALLOW GOD TO CHANGE US.

Leaning in requires us to change our posture, give up our crutches, and allow God to change us. And when we create the habit of leaning in, we find God in unexpected places. When we lean in to relationships, conversations seem to flow more freely. When we lean in to situations, divine appointments can occur. When we lean in to God's presence, we open our hearts to new revelations of His love for us. When we lean in to His Word, every time, we find Him faithfully waiting to speak to us.

Say it Again:

- Your physical posture matters because it can direct your emotional and mental posture.
- You can control whether you are leaning in or leaning out of life.
- Your lean will determine your direction.
- Your lean will expose your attitude.
  - › Your attitude is your settled way of thinking or feeling about someone or something.
  - › You can adjust your attitude by changing your lean, your outward behaviors.
- Mission requires us to lean in.
- As Christians we choose to lean into specific things:
  - › Christ: spending time with Jesus every day is essential for a Jesus-follower.
  - › Community: we are not meant to do life alone.
  - › Worship: when we intentionally engage in worship, we are instructing our whole being (body, mind, and spirit) to focus on God. This resets our attitude and our lean.
  - › Bible: the scriptures are ALIVE with HOPE!
- Leaning in to the future reminds me that the best is yet to come and changes my expectation for what God has in store for me!
- Leaning in to challenges, rather than shrinking back, gives me courage for the inevitable fights of life.
- What keeps me from leaning in?
  - › Losses: Focusing on losses causes me to put the emphasis on what cannot be changed and miss the value of the lesson, which can change everything in the future! If I am constantly leaning on my losses to excuse moving forward or my lack of progress, I will not be able to lean in to the next season.
  - › Emotions: My emotions are important messengers but terrible leaders in my life. When I lean into my emotions and

allow them to dominate me, I miss out on leaning in to the firm foundation of truth and consistency.

> › Old Approaches: what you used to do is not necessarily what you should do now. Relying on yesterday's way without evaluation keeps you from leaning in to the new that can move you forward towards your mission.
> › Normal: Jesus didn't die to give us a normal life but the abundant life. There is more!

- Leaning in will change your life. The life of leaning in is a life full of adventure.

Make it Personal:

- Could it be that you are missing something important in life because you aren't leaning in?
- Has leaning into God's word, preaching, and worship become a habit?
- What is one action that you could take this week to change your lean?
- What might happen if you changed your posture?
- Are you expecting God to do great things in the future?
- What do you need to let go of in the past to move into what God has next for you?
- What are you leaning in to today?
- Is your lean taking you in the direction that you want to go in your relationships, your faith, your career?
- What is one thing you'd like to lean in to today that would change your direction going forward?

WE GROW INTENTIONALLY

Intellectual growth should commence at birth and cease only at death.
—ALBERT EINSTEIN

Growth is the great separator between those who succeed and those who do not. When I see a person beginning to separate themselves from the pack, it's almost always due to personal growth.
—JOHN C. MAXWELL

Growth and self-transformation cannot be delegated.
—LEWIS MUMFORD

We grow intentionally or not at all. Children seem to grow without any effort. Of course, there is quite a bit of intention that goes into that growth as any young parent will agree. Feed them, put them in the right place, let them sleep for sufficient lengths of time, and they will grow. They grow taller, stronger, wiser, and more active. Removing those crucial inputs of care has disastrous and heartbreaking results. And that is the case for all of us, all of our lives. It is the level of intention and who is responsible for our crucial life-giving inputs that must be adjusted as we get older. The same actions will not produce the same level of growth. And we cannot rely on others to baby us, providing everything we need to grow through adulthood.

YOU ARE RESPONSIBLE FOR GROWING WHAT GOD GAVE YOU.

We grow intentionally becomes a habit when we embrace and take responsibility for the daily effort necessary to become everything God has called us to be. Growth requires effort. You are responsible for growing what God gave you. That doesn't happen through desire but through decision.

Jesus has a passion for production. We see this through His parables and through His words in the gospels. He told stories about investment and preparation and ultimately left His disciples with the challenge to go into all the world and make disciples. He does not say, "Try your best." No! He told us to go and do something great. Grow the kingdom of God! Be intentional.

GROWING INTENTIONALLY WILL COST ME SOMETHING

Growth is painful. Change is painful. But, nothing is as painful as staying stuck where you do not belong.
—N. R. Narayana Murthy

There is no substitute for hard work.
—Thomas Edison

Growing will demand your time, attention, vulnerability, discomfort, and hard work. However, growing intentionally isn't just about gathering information. On the contrary, increasing your knowledge without allowing that knowledge to change the way you think will lead to more frustration than transformation. If we want to truly grow into a new person, a better person, a more effective person, we have to grow in the way we perceive, interpret, and act in the world. As Christ-followers, we must allow God to change us by changing the way that we think.

So before you begin, ask, "What am I willing to pay?" We don't pay the whole price for following our dreams, for building a life we want to live, for living a life of service up front. No, instead, we pay moment-by-moment and day-by-day. We must embrace the sometimes-slow process of growing.

GROWTH IS A PROCESS, NOT A DESTINATION.

This slow process is also called discipleship. We like to say that discipleship is the process to progress. What does that mean? It means that growth does not usually happen in a huge leap. Instead, it requires patience to take one step at a time. Improvement is the hallmark of intentional growth. To change my direction, my future, my daily routine, I am fighting against a lifetime of habits that are creating a current against me. Now I want to create these new habits. I want to grow intentionally. And that will only happen through repetition over time. Growth is a process, not a destination.

PROCESS OF GROWTH

Strength and growth come only through continuous effort and struggle.
—Napoleon Hill

Growth has a process. Different people describe it differently, but the process is basically the same. You have to absorb new information through experience or communication that leads to a new perspective or way of evaluating your current reality, which in turn leads to doing something in your life differently on a repetitive basis. And this result is growth in an area of your life. As you can see, the process is not a one-time thing. It is only effective as a habit. Thus, the habit: we grow intentionally.

///

SO YOU MAY ONLY SEE THE TRANSFORMATION IN ME, BUT I KNOW THAT BENEATH THE SURFACE ARE SPECIFIC AND INTENTIONAL ACTIONS.

\\

Keith Craft says it this way: we intentionally and constantly gather information, we ask ourselves what this means and begin to put it into practice (maturation), and this leads to transformation. He draws a triangle to show the relationship between these two ongoing and constant processes. Information combined with maturation lead to transformation, at the pinnacle of the triangle, or in our terms growth. Both gathering information and putting our conclusions about the information into practice are intentional. So you may only see the transformation in me, but I know that beneath the surface are specific and intentional actions.

Peter Piñon, a cognitive coach and counselor, created his own decision cycle for clients.[22] It starts with awareness which leads to evaluation and then to management. Management leads to more awareness, and so on and so on we grow. Here is an example. If I become aware that the food I am feeding my child has an impact on their behavior, then I will evaluate my meal planning differently. I discover then that I am not feeding them enough vegetables, and their diet is too full of sugar. I begin to manage this information by adjusting the foods that we have in our home and offer at our table. This management leads to more information, evaluation, and then management of the conclusion. Our family grows healthier as the process works in our lives.

I replaced the word management with a word I'm more familiar with as a coach— practice—and named it the growth cycle. I like the word practice because it conveys that I will not get it "right" the first time. So, we grow intentionally by raising our awareness, evaluating that new awareness, and then practicing the newly chosen behavior or pattern until it becomes a habit. And the cycle goes on and on.

Maybe you are like me, and just the description of this cycle is raising your awareness of some shortcomings in your growth process. I find that people often get stuck at one place or another. Let's go through each part of the process and talk about how to make sure that the process works for you in your life.

INFORMATION AND AWARENESS

In Adam Grant's book, *Think Again*, he explains that it isn't enough to sit in the same pond of information and expect growth. We must expose ourselves to new sets of information, new environments if we want to grow. Keith Craft speaks about the rooms that we choose to live our lives in. Jesus talked about new wineskins. The bottom line is that we can't sit still in the same and expect change. Albert Einstein once defined insanity as doing the same thing over and over again and expecting new results. If we want to raise our awareness, we must do something different, and different often requires intentionality.

We often do not recognize the classrooms of growth in our lives. Most are not as clearly marked as the first-grade class where we learned how to read or the high school lab where we dissected frogs. Many of the most important classrooms of life are hidden from plain sight. And sometimes, they are hidden in the most difficult of seasons. "Consider it pure joy, my brothers and sisters, whenever you face trials of many kinds, because you know that the testing of your faith produces perseverance. Let perseverance finish its work so that you may be mature and complete, not lacking anything" (James 1:2–4 NIV). The classroom of difficulty is a place where we can grow into maturity if we have cultivated the habit of growing intentionally.

GOD USES EVERYTHING TO GROW ME INTO
MATURITY WHERE I WILL HAVE ALL THAT I NEED.

Growing intentionally means that I am constantly looking for what God is teaching me, doing in me, producing through me in every situation, however unlikely. Everything does not happen for a reason, but God uses everything for the good (Romans 8:28). And God uses everything to grow me into maturity where I will have all that I need.

This book is a perfect example of information raising awareness through intentional action. You chose to pick it up, start reading, keep reading. And as you read, maybe you are finding new ideas or being reminded of old ones. Hopefully, you are raising your awareness of the importance of missional living and the possibility that you can change your life through creating and maintaining new habits. This is the process that naturally happens when we put ourselves in the place to be exposed to new information. Maybe you pick up a new book, subscribe to a new blog, attend a church service, or register for a conference. Even a simple coffee shop conversation with a friend can result in the new information that raises our awareness of what is going on and what is possible.

> ## BEST PRACTICE FOR LIVING A LIFE OF INTENTIONAL GROWTH IS TO LIVE A LIFE OF INTENTIONALLY TAKING IN NEW INFORMATION.

Best practice for living a life of intentional growth is to live a life of intentionally taking in new information. In his book, *Ready, Set, Grow*, Scott Wilson explains how he transformed his church staff and eventually his church by requiring intentional reading and podcasts. Why would this be transformative? Because if you expose people to new information, you raise their awareness and assist them on the first step of intentional growth and development.

EVALUATION

Information and awareness alone will not lead to transformative growth. We must also take the next step and evaluate our newfound awareness.

Americans are information junkies. We have 24-hour news, more books than you can imagine at our fingertips, social media, a sea of bloggers, and magazines on every topic imaginable. Yet, all this new information isn't leading to a more educated populace.[23] It is one thing to take in information. It is another to allow it to raise your awareness. Growing up, my father-in-law called this the difference between information and revelation. That is a super-Christian way of saying that you can be informed without having your awareness engaged. So, what is the difference? The difference is whether I am reading, listening, observing with a growth mindset. If I am looking to grow, then it will be easier for information to translate into awareness.

A GROWTH MINDSET IS THE HIGHWAY BETWEEN AWARENESS AND EVALUATION.

For example, if I read about the effects of diet on behavior without a growth mindset, I might find it interesting. The growth cycle will stop there with information. If I am reading with a growth mindset, then this information will cause me to evaluate how the information applies to my own life and family. A growth mindset is the highway between awareness and evaluation. I must live with a commitment to growth so that evaluation can translate the new information I absorb into new practices that I can implement.

As we evaluate new information, we need a lens or filter to assist us in maximizing our growth.

1) **What am I really becoming aware of here?** I can read a book about marriage and feel invigorated by the new content. However, I will not be able to use it effectively to benefit my marriage if I don't know what is exciting me and what I have really learned about myself or the world. For example, the book may have made you aware of the possibility of a better marriage. It might also have shown you gaps in your communication style. Still another option might be that you saw a model or trend that sounded fun, like

fancy date nights, that you'd like to try. What you are becoming aware of will help you answer the next question.

2) **What am I trying to improve or fix?** If we become aware of one area of our business or personal life that is lacking, or something we aren't doing, that doesn't mean that everything is broken. Being specific in our evaluation of what we are trying to fix will assist us in determining the amount of energy to give to change and in ranking which changes should be prioritized in our lives.

3) **What is it going to take?** This is where a plan of action comes together. If it is a new business culture you desire, one that emphasizes grit and gratitude, then maybe a 360-degree survey is the first step, or weekly culture talks. If you want to be healthier in mind and body, since you've learned the connection between diet and behavior, maybe it is only eating desserts on Saturdays or Sundays. If you have realized you are thinking a lot of negative thoughts leading you to a dark emotional place, maybe the action step is adding a daily declaration to your morning routine. Notice I said step because you cannot change everything all at once. Growth is a process!

EVALUATION IS TRANSLATING INFORMATION INTO CHOSEN ACTION OR EVEN INACTION.

Evaluation is translating information into chosen action or even inaction. It is the internal motion before the outward motion. Don't stop there. Take your evaluation, your new plan, your next step, and put it into practice.

PRACTICE

I love the word practice because it communicates that we will try and fail and try again. John Maxwell says, "Sometimes we win, sometimes we learn." Practice allows us to put into place the action that we chose in our evaluation. However, practice also raises our awareness, leads to better evaluation, and more effective practice in the future. It is a cycle. For example, you might adjust the amount of sugar or caffeine in your diet in response to information on the connection between diet and behavior. You will find the level that works best for you and gives you optimum results through several rotations through the cycle. No part is more important than the other. It all works together to create a new way of living and thinking!

> IT IS NOT ABOUT MY DESIRE TO GROW. IT IS
> ABOUT MY DAILY DECISION TO GROW.

Remember, it is not about my desire to grow. It is about my daily decision to grow. Intentional growth is a commitment to practice.[24] There are people who would love to say they ran a marathon, but they don't want to train for one. There are people who would like to play the piano but do not want to practice their scales. There are people who desire a new career but won't work on their sales techniques. Even closer to home, some of us want a great marriage but aren't willing to work for a great marriage. Some want to live a life that lives on but aren't willing to work to build that secure foundation. Some want to do great things but don't want to endure great difficulty. Practice is required to grow intentionally.

THE ENVIRONMENT OF GROWTH

One of the many wonders of the world is the modern greenhouse. In the middle of winter, a greenhouse can set the proper conditions for growing tomatoes. Outside the greenhouse, the tomatoes would most certainly die. Inside, they flourish. Why? Environment.

When God decided to create humanity, He first created an environment. Our environment is carefully tuned to create exactly the right balance of chemicals and gases we need to not only survive but also thrive. Environment matters.

IF WE WANT TO GROW INTENTIONALLY, WE MUST ALSO PAY CLOSE ATTENTION TO OUR ENVIRONMENT.

If we want to grow intentionally, we must also pay close attention to our environment. We have a choice to take responsibility for our environment. Most people simply accept the environment around them. Others know that they can create a greenhouse within and around them tailor-made for personal growth. When you decide to start building a metaphorical greenhouse in your life, you are setting yourself up for intentional growth.

What does that look like? It's easy to start with the parts of our environment that we don't control, like the way our boss speaks or the lack of leadership training in our school. We can start with our parent's choices to raise us a certain way or the tragedies we've experienced in life. Any of these might be enough to stop you from growing and becoming. After all, they are as out of your control as the weather. That is the magic of the greenhouse. What you are creating on the inside doesn't have to depend on the usual suspects on the outside.

HOPE IS SIMPLY SEEING A POSSIBILITY THAT YOU DID NOT SEE BEFORE AND BELIEVING IT IS POSSIBLE FOR YOU!

First, we need to surround ourselves with inspiration. The first step on any growth journey is hope! And hope is simply seeing a possibility that you did not see before and believing it is possible for you! The greenhouse of inspiration intentionally focuses on stories of inspiration, people who did great things, ideas for different ways to live your life, and above all a focus on what God says is possible. He has said it is possible to live in peace, joy, strength, no matter the circumstance. Another verse says that he prepares a table in the presence of our enemies. That looks like greenhouse living to me. Write down quotes, maybe even from this book, that inspire you. Put them on your mirror and start building the greenhouse of inspiration.

Second, we can invite accountability. That might seem counterintuitive since I earlier said the greenhouse doesn't depend on anyone. Here is what I mean. Create a system of accountability by writing down how you are seeking to grow in detail. If you want to get healthy, don't just write down the number of pounds you want to lose; write some healthy choices you want to make. Then, review those choices on a daily or weekly basis. This will provide some personal accountability. If you have a person you trust in your life, invite them in and share your dream or growth steps with them. Report your progress and empower them to ask how you are doing. You can always choose someone else later on if they aren't a good fit. Don't get stuck; build the accountability into your greenhouse so you can grow!

CELEBRATION HELPS TO CEMENT IN YOUR OWN MIND THE POSSIBILITY FOR GROWTH!

Next, build some encouragement and celebration into your routine. Encouragement is when we notice and call out any improvement no matter how small. If you wanted to walk 5,000 steps a day instead of 1,000, but you only did 3,000, encourage yourself! You improved. Celebration is when you meet the standard. Never let a standard or goal, no matter how small, be met without celebration. Celebration helps to cement in your own mind the possibility for growth!

Finally, you need to check your circle. You can build a great greenhouse, but if your life is just full of people constantly leaving the door open and letting the air in and out, it will be hard for things to thrive.

I'm not saying you should abandon your friends or family, although boundaries can be a good thing. I am saying that everyone needs a circle that wants to grow with them. You might have to join a mastermind or business group in your town. Maybe you need to identify a few friends and set up a monthly dream accountability lunch. Whatever you do, don't do this journey alone. The internet has made community possible for just about everyone. If the first community you try doesn't work, try again. And if all else fails, create the community you wish you had!

GROWING INTENTIONALLY AS A CHRIST-FOLLOWER

Growing intentionally as a Christ-follower is simple, but it is not easy. We read our Bible, we pray, and we put into action God's way. It is simple. Every day, we read, pray, and practice. Read. Pray. Practice. Repeat for a lifetime. This life of devotion leads to a lifetime of discipleship. And the life of devotion must be done in community. Why? Because community is where we practice the most important of all of Jesus' commands. "Love others the way I have loved you." Isolated Christian devotion cannot produce in us love because love is tested, tempered, and finally transformed in community.

To grow intentionally, we must be committed to study. Leaders are learners.[25] Therefore, leaders are readers. If you say, "Well, I'm not a leader," you are wrong. You lead yourself every single day. Study God's word. Read other books. Learn to lead yourself well. Books are really shortcuts to knowledge. Someone else has done the work, and you get to benefit. If you want to grow intentionally, set a goal of books to read for the month or year and stick to it. I've seen what reading growth-oriented books can do for individuals, and it is truly astounding. A commitment of a few hours a month could change your life.

There are also lots of free resources for study. Blogs, podcasts, and email newsletters will bring information to your inbox or mobile phone. What area do you want to grow in? Parenting? There are resources for that. Experts, who love God's words and are passionate about childhood development, will coach you right from the comfort of your own home. Marriage? So many resources can help you improve communication, learn how to deal with different personalities, and fall in love again with your life partner. Business? Health? Resources for that too. World-class personal trainers will lead you in a workout on your TV or smartphone. Faith? So many resources. It does not matter your challenge. If you put in the time to study, you can grow past your challenges into a champion.

SERVING IS WHERE OUR INTERNAL GROWTH IS PUT TO THE TEST.

If we want to grow intentionally, we must also be committed to serving. Serving others is always productive preparation. Serving breaks down our selfish tendencies and opens us to new ideas. Serving breaks down our pride and reminds us that we don't have all the answers. Serving breaks down our excuses and forces us to rely on others. Serving can grow you in areas that study never will. It is the outworking of inward knowledge. Serving is where our internal growth is put to the test.

SERVING GROWS US BY MOVING US FROM OUR COMFORT ZONE TO OUR GROWTH ZONE.

Often people who are stagnant in their faith find new purpose and begin to grow intentionally because they begin to serve. Within our own church community, some of them serve in the ministry to foster care families; others are passionate about administration; still others teach classes to women exiting the sex industry. It does not matter where you serve, only that you serve with your whole heart. Serving grows us by moving us from our comfort zone to our growth zone. And yes, serving is often quite uncomfortable. The sooner you can get comfortable with being uncomfortable, the faster you can grow.

Growing intentionally will also require a commitment to community. We grow faster when we are living in a community of people committed to growing intentionally. I love when people ask me what I'm reading these days. It pushes me to have an answer. I love when my small group shares about where they are serving. It pushes me to serve more. I love when I am challenged by teaching to rethink my preconceptions. I begin to grow past my past. You need community. And so do I. Placing yourself intentionally in a growing, thriving community is a great start to personally growing intentionally.

As a church, we also grow intentionally. We are not getting bigger by accident. We are not surprised by the growth. We intentionally create services that are accessible to people who are new to the faith. We intentionally create a social media presence that would be attractive to those looking for a church home. We intentionally encourage personal invitation. We intentionally prepare our church house every week for visitors. And we follow up with the intention that God has put them in our path for this season for a reason. Growth happens intentionally, and we have decided to be intentional together.

Instead of blaming circumstances, I encourage you to take an honest look at your life, your organization, your church and ask, "Where have we stopped growing?" Growth isn't just about numbers. It is also about health. It just so happens that most of the time healthy things grow. If you don't know the next step to help you grow intentionally, ask someone. Get help. Find a coach. Go to counseling. Attend a seminar or conference. And then apply what you are learning. It is amazing to find that what we intentionally seek to grow most often will grow.

If you want to grow intentionally, take it a step further and set trackable goals, have a method for tracking your progress, and monitor your progress daily. For example, you might adopt a Bible reading plan, get an app, and mark off each chapter as you read it. You would then be able to track your progress on the app to see if you are improving in consistency and quantity. You might pick up a journal and use a method like SOAP (Scripture, Observation, Application, Prayer) in your devotional time. (If you don't know the SOAP method, I encourage you to look it up! It's a really helpful way to read and study the Bible on a personal basis.) You might join a Bible study and use the community to keep you accountable. None of these methods require a lot of time, money, or sophistication. They all require intentionality. All will result in growth for you!

GOD DID NOT GIVE US CHAIRS, BUT HE POPULATED THE EARTH WITH TREES.

In John, chapter fifteen, Jesus explains that we cannot produce fruit, we cannot grow without staying connected to Him. "I am the true grapevine, and my Father is the gardener. He cuts off every branch of mine that doesn't produce fruit, and he prunes the branches that do bear fruit so they will produce even more" (John 15:1–2 NLT). We cannot produce fruit apart from God, but God does not produce the fruit for us. Instead, He gives us what we need to grow and produce fruit. God did not give us chairs, but he populated the earth with trees. If we are faithful as Christ-followers to stay connected to him as the source of all things, to embrace the hard work of the process, and never give up, we will find that intentional growth will become a cornerstone habit in our lives.

DAILY HABITS OF SUCCESS WILL MAKE SUCCESS A DAILY HABIT.

Say It Again:

- ◆ Intentional Growth is a habit that must be cultivated.
- ◆ It starts with taking personal responsibility for your growth. No one else will do the work for you!
- ◆ Warning: growing intentionally will cost you. The rewards outweigh the costs in the long run.
- ◆ There is a process to growth. We call this discipleship—the process to progress.
  - › Awareness – increasing what we know about ourselves and the world around us opens up new possibilities. This process can be challenging, but it is crucial to intentional growth.
  - › Evaluation – when we not only take in information but also ask, "How does this apply to me?" we are able to leverage information into transformation.
  - › Practice – this is where we take the action steps from our evaluation and put them to the test. We expect failure and readjustment as the cycle continues to feed into itself.
- ◆ Growing also requires a proper environment. The good news is that we are all capable of building our own greenhouse of growth.
  - › Our greenhouse begins with inspiration. We need hope to help us move forward. Inspiration shows us what is possible. Hope is when we make it personal.
  - › Our greenhouse gets even stronger with accountability. Personal accountability comes from writing our goals and growth steps. Then we can share with others to create another layer of accountability!
  - › We also want to intentionally inject encouragement and celebration into our routines. Encouragement for any bit of progress. Celebration for when we meet our goals and standards! Both come together to give us energy on the journey.

› Finally, our greenhouse needs the right community or circle to thrive. Intentionally choose people who are on their own growth journey. We go farther together!

Make it Personal:

- How are you growing intentionally right now?
- Think of an area where you would like to grow this year.
- What is the next step you could take to intentionally grow in that area?
- Where have you given up on growing? Why? Ask God to help you see beyond your own limitations into what He has for your future.

WE PRACTICE HONESTY

Honesty is the fastest way to prevent a mistake from turning into a failure.
—JAMES ALTUCHER

Honesty is more than not lying. It is truth telling,
truth speaking, truth living, and truth loving.
—JAMES E. FAUST

Honesty and integrity are absolutely essential for success
in life - all areas of life. The really good news is that
anyone can develop both honesty and integrity.
—ZIG ZIGLAR

HONESTY IS DIFFICULT. BEING HONEST WITH YOURSELF IS ONE OF THE HARDEST THINGS YOU WILL EVER DO IN LIFE.

The tendency when practicing honesty is to start on the outside by being honest with others. I can remember the first time we introduced this idea at church. A woman walked up to one of our pastors after service glowing and said, "I can't wait to go and practice on my husband!" She had missed the point. Honesty starts with me.

We all want to start with everyone else because their problems seem so clear! If the world would just do what I think is best, then everyone would be just fine. When Destiny and I first were married, I really felt called to practice honesty . . . with her. I wanted to help her correct every single aspect of her life that I saw as less than optimum. Surprisingly, this did not go well. And she even had some suggestions for me! Can you believe it?

The problem is when we start by practicing honesty on the outside, we don't yet have the proper perspective to be effective. Jesus gives us the pathway, the step-by-step manual for practicing honesty. "Do not judge others, and you will not be judged. For you will be treated as you treat others. The standard you use in judging is the standard by which you will be judged. And why worry about a speck in your friend's eye when you have a log in your own? How can you think of saying to your friend, 'Let me help you get rid of that speck in your eye,' when you can't see past the log in your own eye? Hypocrite! First get rid of the log in your own eye; then you will see well enough to deal with the speck in your friend's eye" (Matthew 7:1–5 NLT).

DEALING WITH YOUR OWN ISSUES WILL GIVE YOU THE PROPER PERSPECTIVE TO DEAL WITH THOSE AROUND YOU.

Jesus is telling us that practicing honesty does not mean judging. Practicing honesty does not mean giving your tongue a license to "go off" on those around you who don't meet your standard. In fact, people who try to practice honesty with others before practicing it with themselves come off judgmental and cynical or even enabling. Practicing honesty starts with dealing with our own issues. You need God. You are imperfect. I need God. I am imperfect. Dealing with your own issues will give you the proper perspective to deal with those around you. This is the pattern for effectively practicing honesty as a habit.

WHERE ARE YOU?

For those of you over forty, do you remember the little red dot that told you the information you needed most at the mall? Let me explain for the younger crowd. Back in the day, prior to cell phones, if you were looking for a certain store in the mall, you would walk in and find the store directory. It wasn't electronic or a touch screen. It was just a sign on a wall or a display. And it had all the stores laid out on a map. The most important part was the red dot that signified "You Are Here!" If you don't know where you are, it is hard to find what you are looking for and to travel to where you are going.

Honesty is about establishing the little red dot in our lives. If we aren't honest about where we are, what is going on right now, how will we navigate to where we want to go? If growth and transformation are a journey, then honesty is your first step to ensure you are going in the right direction.

> ### HONESTY IS NOT EASY. HOWEVER, IT IS WORTH FIGHTING FOR.

Honesty can be defined as adherence to the facts or fairness, straightforwardness of conduct.[26] It is not simply a habit of the mouth but the hands and heart. Honesty takes practice. We don't get the hang of it right away. It feels so foreign. It takes practice being honest with ourselves. It takes practice being honest with others. There is give and take. Honesty is not easy. However, it is worth fighting for. And it is a core habit in our house.

WHAT DO YOU BELIEVE?

If we want to practice honesty, we have to first confront our own beliefs. What we believe about ourselves, God, community, life, will affect our way of being, our behavior, and ultimately what we are building in our lives. We will investigate these three honesty-building beliefs throughout the rest of this chapter.

- First – I have issues.
- Second – Those issues are causing me pain.
- Third – I need help.

If you don't believe these three things about yourself, then it will be almost impossible to begin practicing honesty as a habit in a healthy way.

Have you ever been fighting with someone over absolutely nothing? You know that you are just mad because it was the worst day ever at work. You know that you are just frustrated because you spilled coffee on your shirt. You know you are still upset with him about the stupid thing he did two days before. And yet, you find yourself acting as though the real issue was the late arrival, improper response, or accidental collision. That is the moment where we have a choice: practice honesty or cling to our fantasy. One will lead to vulnerability, humility, and often peace. The other to feeling self-satisfied in the short run but miserable in the long run.

We practice honesty because it allows us to be vulnerable, to stop the cycle of anger and rage, to embrace those around us—and even ourselves—with grace. Honesty peels off the layers that we create to protect ourselves from the outside world. It breaks down the walls, the excuses, the coping mechanisms. Honesty forces us to look deeply into our own hearts and confront the good, bad, and ugly that live within us. Vulnerability is not a weakness; it is a strength that allows us to connect to the world around us in a deeper way. Brene Brown says, "When we find the courage to share our experiences and the compassion to hear others tell their stories, we force shame out of hiding, and end the silence."

PRACTICING HONESTY WILL UNCOVER THINGS ABOUT YOURSELF THAT ARE NOT PRETTY AND YOU MAY NOT BE VERY PROUD OF.

I must begin this journey of practicing honesty by realizing, anticipating, believing, and knowing that I am not perfect. Don't begin practicing honesty expecting to find all roses and lollipops. Practicing honesty will uncover things about yourself that are not pretty and you may not be very proud of. Ask yourself some hard questions. If you can't think of any, google self-examination questions on the internet to get some ideas.

Oftentimes, we are afraid of what practicing honesty will expose in us. Honesty reveals things in us that we wish weren't there! Yet, the heart of Christianity is that we are all sinners. We all fail. We all have issues. We all have dysfunction. It is okay to struggle; just be honest. Somehow, nothing seems quite as scary in the light as it does in the dark.

Jesus said that those who are forgiven a lot will love Him a lot (Luke 7:36–39; 44–47). And here lies the problem. No one has been forgiven just a little bit! We are all sinners. We have all been forgiven more than we deserve. It is only our perceptions, our lack of honesty, that keep us from understanding the depth of our own sin. It is when we are honest about our own issues that we realize how much we have been forgiven and truly fall in love with Jesus again.

HONESTY IS DIFFICULT BECAUSE IT FORCES US TO CONFRONT OURSELVES.

Honesty is difficult because it forces us to confront ourselves. It is easier to blame others or complain about those around us. However, if we just blame and complain, we won't take responsibility for the one thing we can change: ourselves! Practicing honesty requires us to confront our own hearts. And we are afraid of what we might find. When we start from the place of understanding our brokenness and falling in love with the Jesus who is our only hope, we will willingly begin to practice honesty. After all, what do I have to lose? I already know that I am a sinner in need of a Savior. I would prefer to have all of my flaws on the table so that Jesus can change every single part of me. Being vulnerable, understanding how much Jesus has done for me, will allow me to better value my neighbor. I will value his struggle, value his heart, value his opinion, and value his attempts to practice honesty with me.

THE ENEMY WANTS TO MAKE SURE WE ARE AFRAID OF EACH OTHER INSTEAD OF UNITED IN LOVE.

Don't allow fear to prevent you from practicing honesty. Honesty is what brings hope, help, and healing. The enemy wants to make sure we are afraid of each other instead of united in love. Yet Paul tells us, "For we are not fighting against flesh-and-blood enemies, but against evil rulers and authorities of the unseen world, against mighty powers in this dark world, and against evil spirits in the heavenly places" (Ephesians 6:12 NLT). We cannot resist the enemy if we turn each other into the enemy. If I am worried about impressing you, it will be difficult to fight beside you.

WHO CAN HELP?

Of course, practicing honesty isn't just about engaging our personal relationship with God or even self-reflection. Getting something out of your eye is almost impossible without a mirror and/or a helper. You need help! I need help! We need help! For Christians, the Bible is our mirror. It teaches us and reveals flaws in our thinking that remove blinders from our eyes. And community is our helper. We should be utilizing both on a regular basis to help us see clearly. Ask others for their perspective. Don't just ask anyone. Ask people you trust who won't just say what you want to hear and instead will help broaden your perspective. Pray and ask for God's perspective. The Holy Spirit convicts and guides and reveals (John 16:8). Just a hint: this works much better if you are reading your Bible regularly.

James, the brother of Jesus, said it this way: "Confess your sins to each other so you can be healed" (James 5:16). Confession, just being honest, brings healing. The power of vulnerability is that we do not have to be understood. We just need to be heard. Vulnerability invites us to a discussion, not a debate. When I am vulnerable with you, I want you to hear me, not judge me. And when you are vulnerable with me, you want to know I understand even if I disagree.

IT'S HARD TO PRACTICE HONESTY, BUT IF YOU WANT TO CHANGE CULTURE, YOU MUST INVITE AND PARTICIPATE IN AWKWARD AND HONEST CONVERSATIONS.

It's hard to practice honesty, but if you want to change culture, you must invite and participate in awkward and honest conversations. Several years ago, our community began having some honest conversations about racism. Those conversations started in living rooms, moved to our auditorium stage, and found their way into foyers and coffee shops. We started to listen to each other and confront an issue that continues to shape the culture around us and even in us. Reconciliation starts with communication but requires a response, repentance. People in our community started asking questions, sharing stories, being honest about their feelings, getting vulnerable with each other. And our internal culture shifted for the better.[27]

When we are willing to be honest with ourselves and invite others into the process, real culture change can begin to happen. And that is why practicing honesty is so crucial to our mission. If we can't find the little red dot, we can't move forward. Sometimes the key to the little red dot is inviting others to point out our blind spots and then being willing to allow community to help us heal and become something different.

NOW WHAT?

When we discussed growing intentionally, we learned about the growth cycle: awareness, evaluation, practice. What do we do with all of the awareness raised through the practice of honesty? Specifically, what do we do when we become aware of areas where we have missed the mark or hurt others? These are areas where we are suddenly and urgently convinced of the need to change.

When Destiny points out a blind spot in my life, my first instinct is always to argue to the end that she is wrong and I am right. I fight against the new awareness with all of my heart. It's the way I'm wired. Sooner or later, I usually realize that she's right. The way I was thinking, the action I took, the words I used fell far short of who I want to be and who God has called me to be. So, I've learned at that moment to start a process that helps me to not only learn from my mistakes but leverage them for lasting change.

First, admit the mistake. Sometimes (always in my case), this is the hardest part. What you are admitting to will determine how much you are able to change and what you are willing to learn. Second, apologize. Here is where you can tell if you are admitting to the right things. "I'm sorry you are upset" is fine if you aren't trying to change anything about yourself. "I'm sorry for not honoring my word by arriving on time. I know it left you to deal with all the details alone, and that wasn't fair" is an apology that you can grow from. Sometimes you need to apologize to yourself because you didn't keep your promise or honor your own boundaries. Take that process seriously as well.

Once you have admitted your mistake and truly apologized, we are only halfway there. I want to stop and state here that you have no control over whether people forgive you. Apologizing doesn't ensure that you will have a person's trust or even favor again. You still should do it because it is an important part of your change process. When we are vulnerable, even if others don't meet us halfway, we open ourselves to real and lasting change.

Next, we want to analyze the mistake. Some mistakes take a quick analysis. I didn't get up on time and therefore made my spouse late because I have created a habit of hitting snooze. It's simple and doesn't take a lot of analysis. Many times, however, our analysis will be deeper and even progressive over time. I am sleeping in because I don't really value morning routines. We keep fighting in the mornings, and I have come to the conclusion it's inevitable. These deeper analyses are great, but the goal is to get to the final step. That step is adjust!

> ## WE ARE AFRAID OF BEING A FAILURE SO WE CANNOT ADMIT THAT WE HAVE TRULY FAILED.

When we make a mistake, when we hurt others, when we fail, there is a tendency to get stuck at every step between admit and adjust. We can get stuck on admit because we allow our mistake to become an identity issue. We are afraid of being a failure so we cannot admit that we have truly failed. We get stuck on the apology. We get stuck in paralysis from too much analysis. Remember throughout the process that it's crucial to move to adjust. Even if you later realize more that you could learn or change, and you likely will, adjusting what you can see, what you do understand, or what your analysis dictates right now is crucial to keep you on the path of change.

WHAT ABOUT OTHERS?

Remember that quote we read earlier from Jesus? Let's read the last line again together: "First get rid of the log in your own eye; then you will see well enough to deal with the speck in your friend's eye" (Matthew 7:5 NLT). Notice that Jesus isn't saying, "Don't help your friend!" Instead, there is an order to things.

After you have gone through the process of practicing honesty with yourself and inviting others into that process, then you can move on to practicing honesty with others. The key here is choosing a loving perspective within relationship. Remember, you are speaking to God's favorite child. This person is valuable to Him. And this person has dreams, aspirations, disappointments, and feelings that are just as real as my own. We practice honesty for the benefit of others and our relationships. We don't just spout off to make ourselves feel better or satisfy a need to be "authentic." Ask yourself, "Am I for this person? How will this conversation help them? Help us? Have I been invited to speak into their life?"

Remember that we build relationships through questions, not statements. Practicing honesty first requires you to better understand the other person's big red dot – where they are in life. If you look at an issue and think, "How could anyone believe that?" take the time to find someone with that belief and ask them. Don't ask and then respond; just ask, thank them, and try to understand what you have learned.

The apostle James understood how hard it is for us to practice honesty. Our tongue doesn't want to be honest (James 3). Our tongue wants to set the world on fire. We cannot tame our tongue. We can train our tongue. We can train our tongue by doing good works. We can train our tongue by listening to the Holy Spirit. We can train our tongue by letting God work on us first. We can train our tongue by maintaining a posture of humility and learning. We can train our tongue to practice honesty, not cruelty. We have twelve House Habits for a reason. Ask yourself: Am I loving big here? Am I protecting unity? Am I honoring consistently? If the answer is no, then we may need to adjust our perspective before practicing honesty with others.

PRACTICING HONESTY EFFECTIVELY CAN STRENGTHEN MARRIAGES, FAMILIES, AND BUSINESSES.

The Bible encourages us to speak the truth in love (Ephesians 4:11–16). It also admonishes us to be kind (1 Corinthians 13; Galatians 5:22–23). Kindness isn't always nice. We are required to engage in kind communication if we want to practice honesty with others. Kind communication is clear and direct. It is not passive-aggressive. Don't expect your friend or spouse to read your mind. Be clear about what is going on, why you are bringing it up, and what you'd like to see changed. Practicing honesty effectively can strengthen marriages, families, and businesses.

Do not confuse your job with His job. Your job is honesty. His job is transformation.

Ultimately, we must trust God. We practice honesty, but we are not in charge of transformation. He is the only one who can make the difference. Do not confuse your job with His job. Your job is honesty. His job is transformation. It takes practice. You aren't always going to get it right. Practicing honesty is worth trying, failing, apologizing, and trying again. And remember to approach every communication with humility because, ultimately, we have a limited perspective. We trust in the Lord and put our hope in Him, not in our own limited understanding.

Say It Again:

- ◆ We practice honesty starting from the inside out.
- ◆ Practicing honesty is the process of determining where we are so we can decide where we are going.
- ◆ Our beliefs are core to our ability to practice honesty.
- ◆ I have issues or problems.
- ◆ Those issues are causing me and others pain.
- ◆ I need help.
- ◆ When we understand we need help, then we can invite God and people into the process to assist us in practicing honesty. Others help us to see the blind spots in our lives.
- ◆ Once we have identified an issue or made a mistake, we then engage in the change process.
- ◆ Admit the mistake in as much detail as possible to yourself.
- ◆ Apologize to the person or persons who were hurt. You can also apologize to your current self on behalf of your past self that made the mistake!
- ◆ Analyze why you made that choice or why your actions had the results they did. Analysis should be as deep as necessary to get you to the next step. However, watch out for overanalysis that leads to paralysis!
- ◆ Adjust something. It might be your environment or thought process, or even goals. Remember that this is a cycle of change. It will take time!
- ◆ Now that you have the proper perspective, you can begin practicing honesty with others in relationship.
- ◆ Remember that you are not responsible for the transformation journey of those around you. Rather, you are responsible for your part—practicing honesty as appropriate within that relationship.

Make It Personal:

- ◆ What does it mean to practice honesty? Why do we need to practice?

- How could you start practicing honesty with yourself?
- Think of three questions that you could ask yourself daily to begin practicing honesty.
- What holds you back from practicing honesty in your relationships? How could beginning to practice honesty help make things better?
- How does loving big and protecting unity help guide the way we practice honesty?
- Ask God to speak to you about areas in your life where you are not being honest. Commit to allow Him to shine his light in even the darkest corners.

WE EMBRACE DISCIPLINE

Discipline is the bridge between goals and accomplishment.
—JIM ROHN

You can tell a lot about relationships by the way people greet each other. Sitting in an airport waiting room provides some of the best people-watching available. Man walks out of security to a gaggle of small children and a wife who wraps herself around him like a long-lost blanket—must have been a long trip. Woman walks out to greet two well-dressed colleagues—handshakes all around—must be a business trip. Teen comes off the plane—adult barely looks up—both walk away in silence—they are merely tolerating each other, and it shows.

WE MUST LEARN NOT MERELY TO TOLERATE DISCIPLINE BUT TO EMBRACE IT.

We must learn not merely to tolerate discipline but to embrace it. Imagine yourself wrapping your arms around discipline, kissing discipline on the cheek, embracing it as a loved one. That should be our relationship with discipline because it is the pathway to the abundant life (Proverbs 10:17). In fact, Proverbs says that it is necessary to embrace discipline in order to learn. Scientists have shown us that our disposition toward learning actually affects our ability to learn.[28] When we endure, we get through it. When we embrace, we get something out of it.

LEARN FROM OTHERS

Discipline is doing what needs to be done even though you don't want to.
—UNKNOWN

///

EMBRACING DISCIPLINE DOES NOT MEAN EMBRACING
OR EVEN TOLERATING ABUSIVE RELATIONSHIPS.

\\

Often, your first experience with discipline is external, not internal. You had parents or teachers or coaches who disciplined you and mentored you. They instructed you in the way that you should go. Maybe you confuse discipline with abuse. It is not the same. Embracing discipline does not mean embracing or even tolerating abusive relationships. Discipline is for your good. And it is not good to accept or stay in an abusive relationship.

Our past experiences with those who disciplined us can influence who we are willing to learn from. The great truth of embracing discipline is that I can learn from anyone if I am willing to discipline my emotions. I do not have to like you or even know you in order to learn from you. I can discipline myself to see past what I do not want to what I do want in any given interaction and turn every situation into a learning experience. Just because someone misused discipline in the past does not mean I cannot embrace discipline as a habit for my life in the future.

When our parents or others in authority discipline us, we often have to choose to obey based on external rewards and consequences. Do your homework and receive good grades. Work hard in practice or run sprints afterward. Learn to sit quietly or go to detention. Discipline isn't pleasant. It is tough. When the trainer tells you to do three more sets, and you really want to lie on the floor and cry, it is easy to hate discipline. Yet we embrace discipline because we know in the end it will lead to good things.

God also disciplines us. And His discipline is always good. I do not believe that God is in the business of punishing His children. Rather, He disciplines them for a purpose. Isaiah says, "Lord, your discipline is good, for it leads to life and health. You restore my health and allow me to live!" (Isaiah 38:16 NLT). Again in Hebrews, we see a picture of God disciplining us for our good. "They (our earthly fathers) disciplined us for a little while as they thought best; but God disciplines us for our good, in order that we may share in his holiness. No discipline seems pleasant at the time, but painful. Later on, however, it produces a harvest of righteousness and peace for those who have been trained by it" (Hebrews 12:10–11 NIV). Embracing discipline results in a new way of living because as we listen to correction, we grow in understanding (Proverbs 15:32). And understanding will change the way we act, speak, think, and behave.

DEVELOP INTERNAL DISCIPLINE

Discipline yourself, and others won't need to.
—John Wooden

When we embrace the external discipline we receive from God and others, then we develop internal disciplines necessary for future success. Paul understood this progression. "Don't you realize that in a race everyone runs, but only one person gets the prize? So run to win! All athletes are disciplined in their training. They do it to win a prize that will fade away, but we do it for an eternal prize. So I run with purpose in every step. I am not just shadowboxing. I discipline my body like an athlete, training it to do what it should. Otherwise, I fear that after preaching to others I myself might be disqualified" (1 Corinthians 9:24–27 NLT). All athletes are disciplined by others but eventually must discipline themselves. Discipline is essential, and embracing discipline is a habit we have to pursue daily if we want to truly fulfill our mission.

EMBRACING DISCIPLINE MEANS EMBRACING THE ETERNAL OVER THE EARTHLY.

Embracing discipline means embracing the eternal over the earthly. Godly discipline isn't just about living a productive life on earth. Godly discipline brings the eternal into our everyday. "Do not waste time arguing over godless ideas and old wives' tales. Instead, train yourself to be godly. Physical training is good, but training for godliness is much better, promising benefits in this life and in the life to come" (1 Timothy 4:7–8 NLT). There are benefits to embracing godly discipline not only in this life but also in the life to come.

Jesus did not only die so that we could spend eternity with Him in heaven. Rather, He died to bring heaven to us. He gave us a new way to live that focused our lives on the eternal. When we embrace discipline, we are making a habit out of choosing what is eternal over what is temporary. We are choosing God's ways, even though they are higher than our ways. We choose rejoicing instead of complaining. We choose thanksgiving over worry. We choose prayer over anxiety. We choose to think good things rather than ponder dark mysteries. We are not naive. No. We are just eternally minded. And we embrace that discipline.

THERE IS NO HABIT THAT IS MORE DIFFICULT TO INTERNALIZE THAN EMBRACING DISCIPLINE.

There is no habit that is more difficult to internalize than embracing discipline. And yet Paul tells Timothy, a young leader in the church, "For God has not given us a spirit of fear and timidity, but of power, love, and self-discipline" (2 Timothy 1:7 NLT). God has given us His Spirit because He wants us to become a disciple.

Jesus explained the call to embrace discipline this way, "[I]f you do not carry your own cross and follow me, you cannot be my disciple" (Luke 14:27 NLT). I think we often overlook how strong this passage really is. Jesus is saying in the strongest of terms, embrace discipline. Discipline is essential. Discipline is the core of being a disciple! If we want to follow Jesus, we will need to make daily choices to take responsibility for what we carry and who we follow. This daily choice requires discipline.

Destiny is not a good driver. I taught her to drive. So, I feel I can be honest about this. She is not a good driver. And her driving becomes even worse when she has to follow someone. Whenever she has to follow me anywhere, I get very, very nervous. Following requires discipline and focus. She isn't focused when she drives. She's thinking about the sky and the music and her passenger and anything except the car in front she is supposed to be following. Sometimes, she even passes me when she is supposed to be following me. We can be just like Destiny. We can have the intention to follow Jesus and lack the discipline to make the small, focused decisions necessary to be His disciple. We can find ourselves passing Him instead of following Him.

EMBRACING DISCIPLINE IS A WHOLE LIFE PROCESS

One summer, Destiny was reading a book by Dallas Willard and, as she often does, decided I should read it too. And by reading it too, I mean that she reads out loud the quotes that matter most regardless of whatever else is going on in the room. This time, I was completely captivated by what she read.

> [N]o one ever says, "If you want to be a great athlete, go vault eighteen feet, run the mile under four minutes," or "If you want to be a great musician, play the Beethoven violin concerto." Instead, we advise the young artist or athlete to enter a certain kind of overall life, one involving deep associations with qualified people as well as rigorously

scheduled time, diet, and activity for the mind and body. . . The secret of the easy yoke, then, is to learn from Christ how to live our total lives, how to invest all our time and energies of mind and body as he did.[29]

YOU BECOME A WORLD-CLASS ATHLETE BY LIVING THE LIFE OF A WORLD-CLASS ATHLETE.

I am an athlete, so I instantly recognized and understood what the author was expressing. You become a world-class athlete by living the life of a world-class athlete. The difference between the average and the elite isn't just their practice routine; it is their whole approach to life. There is no off-season. There is no clocking in and clocking out. Becoming an athlete or musician is a lifestyle, not just a career path. And here, the author was explaining that Christianity requires the same lifestyle approach, only for one's whole life.

In reality, embracing discipline is a lifelong process. We start off afraid of the pain of change or the pain of pushing ourselves beyond our perceived limits. Then, we have a breakthrough. The discipline, whether practicing the piano or prayer, moves from being an enemy to a friend. We see how stretching or running or fasting has begun to shape our lives for the good. And then, we are faced with maintaining the current discipline while embracing and optimizing the next. It is a lifelong process of converting the enemy of discipline into the friend, of choosing to value and embrace the gain of discipline in the moments we are enduring the pain.

This mindset is necessary for growing intentionally, practicing honesty, loving big, and all the rest. This habit is required for anyone who would change their life and become more than they are today. And for the disciple of Christ, it is absolutely essential that we embrace discipline, not as a way to heaven, but as a way to become more like our Savior. And that, my friend, will take our entire life. So, don't get tired as you find there are days when embracing discipline is easier than others.

Keep seeking to draw discipline close, embracing the process, and allowing God to use discipline in your life to make you into a disciple.

THERE ARE THREE AREAS WHERE WE MUST EMBRACE DISCIPLINE

EMBRACE DISCIPLINE IN OUR THOUGHTS.

Success is not a matter of mastering subtle, sophisticated theory but rather of embracing common sense with uncommon levels of discipline and persistence.
—Patrick Lencioni

WHATEVER YOU THINK ABOUT, YOU WILL BE ABOUT.

Whatever you think about, you will be about. If you think about the eternal things, you will live for the eternal things. Paul makes a direct connection between embracing discipline in our thoughts and our focus on the eternal. "Since you have been raised to new life with Christ, set your sights on the realities of heaven, where Christ sits in the place of honor at God's right hand. Think about the things of heaven, not the things of earth. For you died to this life, and your real life is hidden with Christ in God" (Colossians 3:1–3 NLT). We cannot find our real life without embracing discipline in our thoughts.

Our thought patterns make a massive impact on our moods, abilities, and even relationships. Yet, we can often neglect embracing discipline when it comes to our thoughts. One practice that has helped me is meditation. Some people say this is an eastern religion thing. It is not. Meditation is all over the Bible. God gave us our breath as a way to help control our physical bodies, but also our emotions and even our perception. An essential element of embracing discipline is slowing down enough to become aware of our thoughts so that we can address those that are not in line with our mission, our beliefs, and our future hopes. Meditation has been a powerful tool for me in learning to do this. I start and end with prayer and use the time in between to relax and learn to listen to what I'm thinking about.

What are you thinking about? How is it affecting the way that you interact with others? Could it be possible that your marriage, your work, your sleep could be improved just by embracing discipline in your thoughts? One of the most important lessons I have learned is that my thoughts are not "me." I choose who I want to be, and I have power to direct my thoughts.

So many issues we deal with every day stem from our thinking. Feelings of guilt, condemnation, shame, fear, feeling unqualified all come from our thoughts. Faith and fear come from the same place— our minds. Faith and fear are both beliefs. One says, "I can." The other says, "I can't!" One says, "God is for me." And the other says, "God shouldn't have picked me." Sometimes it is less clear-cut, and we need help identifying the thinking that is causing us to keep from moving forward or introducing unnecessary fear into our lives. For many years, every time Destiny answered the phone from her boss, she would think, "What's wrong? What did I do?" This kind of thinking made her nervous and worried even when there was nothing to worry about. When she identified her negative thought pattern, she then had to embrace the discipline of replacing those thoughts. She would choose to look at the ringing phone for a moment and intentionally think, "I'm excited to be a help today. I am a great resource for this company, and that is why my boss is calling." It changed her mentality from fear to confidence over time, but it took embracing discipline instead of justifying the old thought pattern.

As Christ-followers, we embrace discipline in our thoughts by reading and meditating on God's words. This is a daily discipline that we must embrace. Reading your Bible isn't a religious duty. Reading the Word of God stimulates wholesome thinking and empowers you to live a life of power, love, and self-discipline (2 Peter 3:1–2). You don't have to start big. Begin by reading for five minutes, ten minutes, fifteen minutes a day, and then spend a few moments thinking about what you have read.

We can also embrace discipline in our thoughts by replacing inputs that focus on the negative with inputs that focus on the eternal. One of the most life-changing small decisions Destiny and I ever made was to cut cable out of our budget. We didn't make that decision as a stance against television. It was a purely financial decision. And yet, we've never gone back. Why? Because Destiny found that removing that input and replacing it with podcasts, God's words, and conversations with our family significantly reduced her level of anxiety. The initial decision wasn't easy, but the benefits of embracing discipline are evident in our home.

CHOOSE TO SPEND TIME WITH THE ONES THAT ELEVATE YOUR THINKING AND GIVE YOU COURAGE.

We embrace discipline in our thoughts by intentionally placing ourselves around those who encourage us to think thoughts that encourage and motivate us rather than tear us down. Do you have friends who refresh you and don't depress you? Do you have friends who strengthen you and don't strangle you? Choose to spend time with the ones that elevate your thinking and give you courage. Choose to spend time with friends that think in a way that moves them forward in life. This requires intention. If you don't have encouraging people in your current circle, issue some invitations. Recruit someone for lunch or coffee or to go for a walk. Look around at people living the life you want to live and ask them questions, discover the way that they think, and then begin practicing those patterns. Sometimes it is easier to be around those who empower your pity party. Don't take the easy route! Embrace discipline. Make it a habit.

EMBRACE DISCIPLINE IN THE WAY WE SPEAK.

We must all suffer one of two things: the pain of discipline or the pain of regret or disappointment.
—JIM ROHN

We also have to embrace discipline in the way we speak. What do you say to yourself? If you said the same thing to anyone else, how would they feel? Would you speak that way to your child, your best friend? We have so many patterns of speech that infect our lives. Embracing discipline in our speech means slowing down and evaluating whether what we are saying lines up with what we believe and where we want to go in life.

In our family, we constantly talk about the power of story. Our words create the narrative that our lives follow. If we are constantly tearing ourselves and others down, it will be an obstacle to moving into the life we want to live and achieving the mission we are called to pursue. Oftentimes, people will dismiss the importance of words by saying, "I'm just teasing." By all means, make me laugh. I love to laugh! I've learned that laughing at the expense of others ultimately isn't worth the momentary joy. Within a family, a business, a church, that kind of humor can have a heavy impact. We can start to create characters for ourselves and others with our humor that are opposite of who we want to become. Embracing discipline in our words means recognizing that they have power and then using that power for good, to build up, and to create the life we want to live.

EXAMINE YOUR SPEECH, THEN EMBRACE THE DISCIPLINE NECESSARY TO BRING IT IN ALIGNMENT WITH GOD'S WORDS.

A daily way to embrace discipline in the way we speak is to write and say declarations. We use declarations as a family every single day. Why? Because it is a discipline that reminds me of how important my words really are. My declaration challenges not only my patterns of speech, but also my internal dialogue. I am forced to confront the areas where what I'm saying about myself doesn't line up with what I believe. Remember, it is not humility to speak poorly of yourself. If you continually speak negatively about yourself to others, even in humor, you will eventually begin to believe what you say. Examine your speech, then embrace the discipline necessary to bring it in alignment with God's words.

EMBRACE THE DISCIPLINE OF TRYING NEW THINGS.

Embracing discipline will ultimately require us to try new things. Maybe it is a new way of thinking, new way of speaking, new way of responding, new way of acting. When I have made a habit of embracing discipline, I have acknowledged that I need discipline and have pre-determined how I will respond when those discipline moments come. I am declaring through my habit that I will choose to be comfortable being uncomfortable.

Practicing doing new things, uncomfortable things, when you don't "need" to helps prepare you for the moment where you will need to step out of your comfort zone in order to accomplish your mission. Think about something new you could try today. Maybe it is as simple as trying a new food at lunch. Maybe it is going out of your way to say hello to someone at work instead of ducking into your office and avoiding the social scene. Maybe it is volunteering with the kids' ministry or greeters even though you are an introvert.

Maybe it is going home and getting the rest you need instead of staying out all night with your friends because you are afraid of missing out. Trying new things is difficult; that is why it is fertile ground for practicing embracing discipline. Trying new things could also just be code for starting. And starting is usually the hardest part of any transformation process.

I encourage you to choose to embrace the discipline of beginning something new. Step out. Start walking every single day. Pray with your kids. Lift your hands during a worship service. Serve your community. Invite someone to church. Have dinner with someone different from you. As Christ-followers, we have to be willing to do things we have never done before or things that we have failed to keep doing in the past, and that requires discipline.

EMBRACING DISCIPLINE IS EASIER IN COMMUNITY

Winners embrace hard work. They love the discipline of it, the trade-off they're making to win. Losers, on the other hand, see it as punishment. And that's the difference.
—Lou Holtz

JUST AS IT IS EASIER NOT TO QUIT IN COMMUNITY, IT IS ALSO EASIER TO EMBRACE DISCIPLINE.

Our church parking lot becomes a gym on many a weekday morning. As early as 5 a.m., Camp Gladiator's many campers run sprints, do exercises, and push themselves to another level of fitness. I walk into church on the same pavement every single week, and that walk contributes almost nothing to my overall health goals. What is the difference? The pavement isn't magic, but the community really is. Just as it is easier not to quit in community, it is also easier to embrace discipline. The community helps you to feel empowered to get one more rep or try to beat your personal best. It is still painful, but the community is there to support you along the way. Besides, as the old adage says, "misery loves company." Shared suffering seems to be easier to bear. And shared victories are so much sweeter. I encourage you to lean in to community as you work to internalize this habit. An anonymous African proverb says, "If you want to go fast, go alone. If you want to go far, go together."

For Christians, the church (globally) is intended to be your engine and accelerator for spiritual growth. And if you read the Bible, you will know that there is no division between what is spiritual and non-spiritual. The community of believers is created by God to "equip [you] for every good work" (Hebrews 13:21). This isn't magic. We can see the same principle in any gym or workout class. Embracing discipline requires creating or entering an environment of transformation. You can create that environment alone, but it is much more difficult. That is why we go to the gym and one of the central reasons we attend and serve at church. Now, it isn't enough to sign up for the right environment. Over 67% of gym memberships go unused.[30] We have to embrace the discipline of the environment in order to get the benefit.

As Christians, we can embrace discipline in our spiritual lives by following the example of the early church. The Book of Acts records that the first believers "devoted themselves to the apostles' teaching, and to fellowship, and to sharing in meals. . .and to prayer" (Acts 2:42 NLT). All of those "exercises" can be done within the context of church. And they are all reflective of the general way that we change as human beings. They were receiving information, evaluating it, and putting it into practice in the context of community. This growth process isn't easy, but we can move towards transformation in strength when we have already decided to embrace this daily discipline. Decide today to stop resisting the pain of leaning in, growing intentionally, and practicing honesty. Instead, wrap your arms around it and choose to embrace discipline so you can see the transformation that you desire in your life.

Say It Again:

- We must embrace rather than merely tolerate discipline.
  - › When we endure, we get through it.
  - › When we embrace, we get something out of it.
- External discipline usually precedes internal discipline.
  - › Just because someone misused discipline in the past does not mean I cannot embrace discipline as a habit for my life in the future.
  - › I can learn from anyone and anything if I am willing to discipline my emotions.
- Internal discipline is a sign of maturity and is necessary for success.
- If we want to follow Jesus, we will need to make daily choices to take responsibility for what we carry and who we follow.
  - › Godly discipline brings the eternal into our everyday.
  - › God has given us His Spirit because He wants us to become a disciple.
- We must embrace discipline in our thoughts.
- We must embrace discipline in our speech.
- We must embrace the discipline of trying new things.
- Discipline is easier to embrace in community.

Make it Personal:

- What does it mean to you to embrace discipline?
- Why must we first embrace discipline internally before we embrace it externally?
- Why is discipline important for a disciple of Christ?
- What are areas of your life where you need to embrace more discipline? What steps can you take today to embrace discipline in those areas?
- What is one difficult thing you can do this week to help develop the habit of embracing discipline in your life?

WE LEAD OUT

Do not go where the path may lead, go instead
where there is no path and leave a trail.
—RALPH WALDO EMERSON

F inally!!! We get to lead! Yes, but leadership requires an even stronger commitment to daily habit formation. Otherwise, we can get distracted by impact results and forget that habits are what will sustain us and whatever we are leading into the next generation. The next four habits, starting with we lead out, are what we call the impact habits. This is where we all really want to start. Impacting the world is the ultimate goal of anyone with a vision, mission, or purpose beyond themselves. We want to see some good exist or some change to happen because of us. The truth is that without connection habits and transformation habits, the impact habits lose much of their power. And even these impact habits require us to not focus on impact results but the daily choices we are making to become the change we want to see in the world. So, with that in mind, let's dive in!

YOU ARE A LEADER. WE ALL ARE.

And as leaders, we choose to lead out. We do not opt out, check out, or sneak out. We lead out.

I lead out of who I am. So, I must learn to lead myself well. If I am unable to lead myself well, then I won't be able to lead others well. Leading out begins with leading myself. It doesn't matter how many leadership books I read or management seminars I attend; if I cannot learn to lead myself, I will fail at leading others.

LEADING YOURSELF MEANS PUTTING INTO PRACTICE WHAT YOU BELIEVE IN AN INTENTIONAL WAY.

What does it mean to lead yourself? Leading yourself means putting into practice what you believe in an intentional way. It is allowing the rest of the house habits to move from your wall to your heart, from the page to a process. Leading yourself is not easy. John Dryden said, "We first make our habits and then our habits make us." That initial making, creation, requires intentionality and hard work. And leading ourselves down the roads that lead to success, happiness, godliness, purpose will take leaning in, growing intentionally, embracing discipline, and practicing honesty. Leading yourself will require you to make a daily decision to let your beliefs and convictions take the lead instead of your emotions and desires.

CHARACTER IS WHAT RESULTS WHEN WE FORCE THE RIGHT ATTITUDE AND ACTIONS OVER TIME.

Leading yourself will require you to force the right attitudes and actions into your life. Character is what results when we force the right attitude and actions over time. Our attitude matters. The incorrect attitude will keep us from taking full responsibility for our lives and, therefore, from leading ourselves successfully. The right attitudes and actions will produce character that can keep us when our gifting fails us.

WE LEAD OUT OF WHO WE ARE

As a leader, the first person I need to lead is me. The first person that I should try to change is me.
—John C. Maxwell

IN ORDER TO SET AN EXAMPLE, YOU HAVE TO
BE AN EXAMPLE. LEADING OTHERS FLOWS
OUT OF HOW YOU LEAD YOURSELF.

Leading yourself is key because it's impossible to create habits to lead others if those habits aren't currently driving your own life. You must first create the habits to lead yourself well because you will only lead others out of who you are. The apostle Paul encouraged young Timothy to set an example for all the believers (1 Timothy 4:12). In order to set an example, you have to be an example. Leading others flows out of how you lead yourself.

YOU HAVE TO BE A DISCIPLE BEFORE
YOU CAN MAKE A DISCIPLE.

Jesus gave us a mission to make disciples (Matthew 28). You cannot make something that you are not. You have to be a disciple before you can make a disciple. The question is not, how do I make disciples? The question is, how do I become a disciple? Because once you become a disciple, you will understand how to make disciples. You will be able to lead out of who you are.

Leading out of who we are can be intimidating. After all, we know ourselves. We know our faults. We know our problems. We know! If we are practicing honesty, then we know we are unqualified to be carriers of God's message and mission. There is a big difference between unqualified and disqualified.[31] Regardless of where we are in life right now, God has decided, through Jesus, to qualify us. The apostle Paul says in Romans that "Because of our faith, Christ has brought us into this place of undeserved privilege where we now stand. . ." (Romans 5:2 NLT). God chose to qualify us for His family and for His mission by sending His son, Jesus. We are justified, sanctified, and qualified through Christ!

WHEN WE HIDE OUR STRUGGLES IN THE DARK, WE SET OURSELVES UP FOR FAILURE AS DISCIPLES AND LEADERS.

Yet, we can still be disqualified. Writing to the Corinthian church, Paul expressed his fear that he would be disqualified (1 Corinthians 9:27). Hidden secrets will disqualify us. When we hide our struggles in the dark, we set ourselves up for failure as disciples and leaders. Sin loves to hide. It loves the dark places. When we choose to lead out, we have to stay honest. Let us be clear: sin does not disqualify us. We are all sinners. Hiding our sin will disqualify us from leading out. It will take our strength and twist our pain into bitterness (Psalm 32:3–5; Psalm 32:1–2). Living in complete honesty with God and in transparency with others creates joy and strength in our lives. Don't hide. Own your struggles. And God will transform your struggle into a story that will set others free.

If we want to lead out, we cannot compare. Leading out means leading out of who we are, not who our neighbor seems to be. You do not know your neighbor. You know yourself. And you are called to run the race marked out for you (Hebrews 12:1). Comparison and judgment go hand in hand. They work together to keep you from leading out. You were created to run your race well, not to judge how well somebody else is running his race. How can you run your race effectively, constantly looking to the right and the left? Don't allow your words and conversations to be occupied with judgment and comparison (Ephesians 4:29; Proverbs 12:12; Proverbs 14:30).

To lead out, you must know who you are. Don't try to lead out like someone else. Know who you are and who God has created you to be. Be honest about your strengths and weaknesses. It is always disturbing to me to listen to singing contests and hear a terrible singer who seems surprised to know that he or she is absolutely terrible. Know your weaknesses, but know your strengths too. Stop trying to be someone else. You be you. Bring your grace gift to the table and lead out of who you are.

> ## NEVER BE CONTENT WHERE YOU ARE. NEVER BE SATISFIED WITH HOW FAR YOU HAVE COME.

To lead out well, you must improve who you are. Once you know who you are, you can make a plan to improve. Never be content where you are. Never be satisfied with how far you have come. Choose to keep reading, keep learning and keep growing. Why? Because if I am going to lead out of who I am, I want to be the best I possibly can. And I know that if I'm breathing, I'm not there yet! Keep improving.

Improving yourself doesn't mean becoming like someone else. Destiny is a speaker, but she doesn't sound like a lot of other women. She preaches like a cross between a professor and an old-time Pentecostal. She can preach the same sermon fourteen times, and it will be different each time. That is who she is. She can flow that way. For me, if I write it on the page, I'm going to say it. And if I preach two sermons back-to-back, the differences will be very minor. We can both improve our speaking ability, but getting better doesn't mean becoming like each other.

It is the same way in leadership. I am a strategic thinker. My thought process when it comes to our church is to point to a destination and trust we can figure out the details along the way. Destiny tends to be systemic. She sees the way every single choice, from where we put the tables to when we take the offering, affects every other piece. And usually, she wants to figure out many of the details in advance. At home, we switch. I need all the details, and she's happy to shoot from the hip. We can both improve, but if I try to think like her, I will be out of my element. If she tries to lead like me, it will be inauthentic. I have to allow change without sacrificing the things that make me great.

THE MISSION CANNOT BE ACCOMPLISHED BY ONE PERSON AND ONE WAY AND ONE GIFT.

To lead out well, you must also lead out of your greatness or your gifting. Great news: you have one! In the letters to the church in Rome and Corinth, the apostle Paul lists in detail the giftings that God has given the church (1 Corinthians 12; Romans 12; Ephesians 4:11–12). Why? He was explaining to them that they each had a part to play in bringing heaven to earth. God had given them all a different piece of the puzzle, a different gift, a different greatness, and a different way of looking at the world. And only when we all come together can we impact the world in the way we want to. The mission cannot be accomplished by one person and one way and one gift. The mission requires each of us bringing who we are, our gifting, to the table.

There is a difference between improving yourself and trying to become someone else. You have to fight to stay true to who you are even when others are trying to make you into something you are not. Why? Because I cannot lead out of who you are. I can only lead out of who I am. The apostle Paul understood that Timothy needed to be himself. He encouraged Timothy to lead out not of who Paul was or his mother was but out of an authentic understanding of self. He encouraged Timothy to use youth as an advantage, to be proud of his heritage, and to teach and encourage the church, not as a proxy for Paul but as a leader in his own right. Don't forget who you are! You be you! God has created you as a unique person to bring your special sauce to the table. And dinner will not taste nearly as good if you bring something bland and generic. Lead out of who you are!

WE LEAD OUT TOGETHER

> *You don't lead by hitting people over the head—*
> *that's assault, not leadership.*
> —DWIGHT D. EISENHOWER

As individuals and as a church, we must lead out of partnerships. Alone, we cannot achieve the mission of Christ. We are invited into partnership with Jesus (1 Corinthians 1:9). And partnership with other Christ-followers makes us stronger. Partnership means I don't just rely on my own resources, wisdom, strength, or power. I can call on the resources, wisdom, strength, and power of my partner to fill in the gaps. We each rely on Jesus for power and wisdom and everything we need. We also need to rely on each other.

As a church, we've decided to lead out in partnerships as much as possible. We do not want to start a new outreach to the homeless. We want to partner with those who are already reaching the homeless community. Before we begin a new outreach or ministry, we look around for who we can join or partner with. Why? Because we are better together! It's not about my thing or your thing; it is about God's thing, this kingdom thing. Leading out is easier and more effective in partnerships.

WE LEAD OUT WITH VULNERABILITY

Vulnerability is scary. Yet it is essential to creating a strong culture. I have found that when Destiny and I share our weaknesses, we encourage others to be strong. Why? Because we all have pain! We all have weakness! As a leader, as a parent, as a boss, share your struggles with those around you. I am always surprised that the stories the people connect with most, which seem to help them move toward Jesus, are my stories of personal failure. The stories I share where I struggled, got angry, and failed are the ones that connect. Why? Because when we lead from a vulnerable place, we are leading out of who we are, not just an image of how we want others to see us. Leading out with vulnerability is allowing God to use what could have destroyed us to build us and build His kingdom.

> ## YOU DO NOT HAVE TO HAVE A PERFECT PLAN BEFORE YOU TAKE ACTION.

As a church we can lead out with vulnerability as well. You do not have to have a perfect plan before you take action. I encourage our staff to lead out by involving people in the process. Don't wait until everything is arranged. Allow people to be part of forming and shaping and planning and doing with you. That is how leaders and culture are created. That is how church planters are born. That is how we translate and transfer culture. If you only allow people into the pretty parts of ministry and missions, you rob them of the lessons that only are learned in the middle of the painful, messy moments.

WE LEAD OUT WITH PERSISTENCE

> ## WE WILL FAIL BUT WILL NOT QUIT.

Leading out requires persistence. It requires continuing steadfastly in the face of opposition. When we establish the habit of leading out, we are resolving to live out Proverbs 24:16 (NLT). "The godly may trip seven times, but they will get up again." I'm not going away. I'm not going to quit or give up. Failure is guaranteed when we choose to lead out. We will fail but will not quit. Instead, we keep putting into practice what we have learned. We keep leading out. Keep improving.

Persistence leads to peace. And when we maintain our peace, we can continue to lead out (Philippians 4:9).

WE LEAD OUT IN OUR FAMILIES

We lead out in our families. Leading out starts in my house, not outside my house. Sometimes leaders can lead out everywhere else except in their homes. This is why leading out of who you are, not a false persona, is so vitally important. When you lead out of what is fake outside of your home, you cannot be real inside your home. And your family knows. When you lead out of who you are outside the home, you will be the same person when you get home. How well are you leading out in your family? You don't have to be the husband or even the parent to lead out in your family. Leading out in your family looks like being an example, telling stories of God's faithfulness, speaking life, serving. Don't overcomplicate it. Lead out in your family. You will make mistakes, but if you are leading out of who you are, God will even use those mistakes. Start today.

WE LEAD OUT INTO THE COMMUNITY

WE ARE NOT A CHURCH IN THE COMMUNITY; WE ARE A CHURCH FOR THE COMMUNITY.

We lead out into the community. At NCC, we are not a church in the community; we are a church for the community. We show we are for the community by inviting them to our house, participating in what matters to them, and by meeting real needs. Because we lead out of partnerships, leading into the community is much easier. Communities are often skeptical about churches because churches sometimes want to take the place of instead of joining with communities. When we decided to reach out to the foster care families of our area, we submitted ourselves to the local foster care bureaucracy. We asked them what they wanted instead of asking them to attend what we wanted to create. When the city wanted to have a family fun day, we sent volunteers. We wore the city's shirts. We didn't promote ourselves. We led out into the community by joining with the community.

WE LEAD OUT FRONT

You see, in life, lots of people know what to do, but few people actually do what they know. Knowing is not enough! You must take action.
—TONY ROBBINS

WE DON'T CREATE A WORLD THAT IS GOOD FOR US; WE INVADE THE WORLD WITH WHAT GOD HAS PUT INSIDE OF US.

We also lead out front. We don't have to be out front. We are willing to join the community and lead out of partnership, but we are unafraid of the front line. Sometimes we have to lead out into the community alone because the gap is just that big. We don't create a world that is good for us; we invade the world with what God has put inside of us. Where is the gap? Is there a partner? Is there something we can join? If not, then I will go first. I will do it first so someone else can do it better. I will care for those who have no one else to care for them. I will fill the gap. I will say yes. Leading out sometimes means leading from the front. Sometimes it means taking the flak. Sometimes it means being the lightning rod. That is why we have to be leading out of who we are. Because when the pressure is on, who we really are comes to the surface.

WE LEAD OUT INTO THE FUTURE

//

THE TRUTH IS, YOU WOULDN'T NEED JESUS TO LIGHT THE PATH IF YOU KNEW THE WAY.

\\

We also lead out into the future. Leading out into the future means embracing the unknown. Leading out into the future means believing the best is yet to come. Leading out into the future means trusting God not just with the world but with our own families, careers, churches, and futures. The unknown is scary because it is unknown. The future can be scary because we aren't sure which way to go or what choices will come our way. The truth is, you wouldn't need Jesus to light the path if you knew the way. Leading out into the future means embracing the lifestyle of Paul. "My life is worth nothing to me unless I use it for finishing the work assigned me by the Lord Jesus—the work of telling others the Good News about the wonderful grace of God" (Acts 20:24 NLT). When we have an eternal perspective, we may not know all the details along the way, but we are sure of who holds the future. So lead out boldly into the future!

Say It Again:

- We are all leaders.
- We lead ourselves every day.
- We lead those around us through influence and experience. Somewhere there is someone who is taking their cues from you. That makes you a leader.
- Leading yourself means putting into practice what you believe in an intentional way.
- Leading out of who you truly are is essential to leading both yourself and others. We choose to own where we are and grow into who we want to be.
- Community is essential to learning to lead yourself and others.
- Our pain does not disqualify us from leading. Instead, it can be a powerful tool in helping us to reach others and learn to lead ourselves.
- We lead out with persistence. Leadership requires us not to give up when things become difficult.
- We lead both those closest to us, our families, and those around us, our community. That doesn't mean we have to always be in charge. Rather, we take the initiative to fill the gaps around us and to support others who are filling gaps.
- Leading will sometimes require us to go first. Don't shrink from that responsibility. Instead, be willing to be the first to try to change something or make a difference.
- We lead out into the future, understanding that someone has to create what comes next.

Make It Personal:

- Do you see yourself as a leader? Why or why not?
- What can you do to lead yourself better today?
- Where have you allowed yourself to lead out of comparison or insecurity instead of confidence?

- How can you lead out into your community? Where are there gaps for you to fill?

WE GIVE GENEROUSLY

Do all the good you can,
By all the means you can,
In all the ways you can,
In all the places you can,
At all the times you can,
To all the people you can,
As long as ever you can.
—JOHN WESLEY

TO BE A GIVER IS A GOOD THING, BUT TO BE A GENEROUS GIVER IS BETTER.

We all know people who give, but not generously. They remind you of their gift on every occasion. They give out of their extreme excess and make sure you know that they have much more than what they gave. They are giving, for sure, but the gift isn't generous. To be a giver is a good thing, but to be a generous giver is better. A generous gift, one that comes from an open heart, makes a difference. It is remembered, not just for what was given, but how it was given, with a spirit of generosity.

That spirit of generosity is what I want you to catch a glimpse of in this chapter. It's not just about action, even though generosity without action is not generosity. It's not just about quantity, even though miserliness and a scarcity mindset are the antitheses of a spirit of generosity. Generous giving is internalizing the statement by Anne Frank, "No one has ever become poor by giving," and beginning to live as though there truly is more than enough. Let's journey together and discover some aspects of this generous spirit that can truly change the world.

GENEROSITY STARTED WITH GOD

For those who believe in Jesus, who follow God, we believe that everything we see in this natural world was given to us and created by God for us. This world is tailor-made for human life. It gives us delicious food, life-giving water, and just the right mix of gases so we can breathe and thrive. And our life here is a gift.

God is a generous giver. I am grateful He did not just give; He gave generously. It's been said you are never more like God than when you give. I'm not sure when we are most like God, but I do know that God is a generous giver. The core of our gospel is this: God gave Jesus, the most extravagant of all gifts, to the world. Why? Simply because He loves us and desires for us to live for eternity with Him (John 3:16). And God continues to give us generous gifts (James 1:17). He gives us peace for anxiety (Philippians 4:6), joy for mourning (Isaiah 61:3), future and hope (Jeremiah 29:11), and so much more. Each of us is given gifts of the Spirit (1 Corinthians 12). God is a generous giver.

And God created us in His image (Genesis 1:27). He made us to be generous givers too. The definition of generous is liberal in giving or sharing; unselfish; free from smallness of mind or character.[32] Isn't that exactly how God has treated us? And if so, then that is the picture of how we should treat each other. We are called to give generously. Generous giving is not a one-time thing. It is not an offering thing. It is not a Christmas thing. Living generous, having the habit of generous giving, comes from becoming a generous person.

GENEROUS PEOPLE ARE GRATEFUL

YOU CAN'T BE GENEROUS WITH WHAT YOU HAVE IF YOU ARE NOT GRATEFUL THAT YOU HAVE IT IN THE FIRST PLACE.

Some of the most generous people I know are also the most grateful. It is hard to be ungrateful and generous. Being ungrateful indicates we either don't have what we want or have less than what we think we deserve. Generosity requires us to acknowledge we have been given so much. You can't be generous with what you have if you are not grateful that you have it in the first place. True gratitude stems from understanding we are all stewards of what we have. We may have worked, but our ability to work comes from God. What we are given, what we earn, the house we live in, does not truly belong to us in the first place. All good gifts come from God. And everything in the earth and on the earth is His. If you want to open the door to be more generous, practice gratitude. Be generous with praise, with thanks, with credit. Give gratitude generously, and then you will be ready to give generously in every area of your life.

GENEROUS PEOPLE ARE INTENTIONAL

If you can't feed a hundred people, then just feed one.
—MOTHER TERESA

Generosity doesn't happen by accident. It demands intentionality. A man in our city believes he has a reputation for being generous because he makes a lot of generous offers. Unfortunately, he rarely comes through. His lack of intention has resulted in a reputation as a miser, the exact opposite of his own perception. You aren't generous because you feel generous. Generosity can be measured. Whether you are generous with your finances is obvious from a quick look at your bank account. Your generosity with time can be seen in your schedule.

Much is made in Evangelical or Pentecostal circles of the value of emotional, spontaneous giving. However, God instructs us to be intentional in our generosity. "Each of you should give what you have decided in your heart to give, not reluctantly or under compulsion, for God loves a cheerful giver" (2 Corinthians 9:7 NIV). What have you decided in your heart? Generosity should be attached to a decision, not just an emotion. I am not generous when I feel like it. Instead, I am generous because I have intentionally decided to make generous choices. I have decided. It is a habit I am cultivating on a regular basis.

Generosity isn't bound by season. Some say, "I will be generous when I get a better job. I will be generous when I get out of this busy season." Some of the people who serve the most faithfully are those with the busiest schedules. And many generous people aren't in the top income brackets. The truth is that if you are not generous where you are, you will likely not be generous when you get to the next season or next promotion. Generosity is a lifestyle, not just a number. Choose to become intentional about your generosity. Make a decision today. Build generosity into your budget, your schedule, your life. Intentionality paves the way for generosity.

GENEROUS PEOPLE ARE FUTURE-FOCUSED

The return we reap from generous actions is not always evident.
—Francesco Guicciardini

IF YOU WANT TO BE A MORE GENEROUS PERSON TOMORROW, BE GENEROUS WHERE YOU ARE TODAY.

Generous people really believe that the best is yet to come. They believe that by being generous, they can make a difference. They can see, imagine, the impact of their generosity. Generosity is an investment in the future. It can be the future of a person, a family, a community, a church. It is always an investment in the future. And those who give generously to God are reinforcing their focus on an eternal future. Jesus tells us that where our treasure is, our heart will follow. If we want to keep our focus on Jesus, on His kingdom, on heaven, then we should choose to live a generous life. As we choose to give, God literally provides for us, increases our resources, and produces in us a great harvest of generosity (2 Corinthians 9:6–12). That means that generosity begets generosity. If you want to be a more generous person tomorrow, be generous where you are today. And God will produce a harvest of generosity in you for the future.

GENEROUS PEOPLE LIVE LIVES FULL OF ADVENTURE

Lose yourself in generous service and every day can be a most unusual day, a triumphant day, an abundantly rewarding day!
—William Arthur Ward

We make a living by what we get, but we make a life by what we give.
—Winston Churchill

The Book of Acts is full of the stories of the most generous of people. In fact, these new believers, the first church, are so generous and so united that they eliminate poverty among their ranks. They share and share alike. They live extreme generosity (Acts 4:32–35). If you want to live a life of adventure, live a generous life. There is nothing boring about generosity. When we make room for the Holy Spirit to move in our lives, when we intentionally allow for generosity in our schedules and our budgets, we open ourselves to adventures beyond our wildest dreams. A generous life is an eventful life. This is the Acts life in action.

IF YOU WANT TO SEE MIRACLES, IF YOU WANT TO LIVE ADVENTURE, LIVE GENEROUSLY.

Jacqueline Randolph has a heart for aged-out foster children. She is a retired lieutenant colonel of the United States Air Force. And she has planned her life and her finances in such a way that she can live her retirement as a self-funded missionary. She has created an intentionally generous life. And she is constantly finding herself in the midst of adventures. One week after letting the local foster care office know she was interested in mentoring at-risk kids, she found herself in not one but two labor and delivery rooms with girls who had recently aged out of the system and were now themselves mothers. One of the girls would likely have died except for Jacque's timely intervention and prompting to take her to receive a prenatal screening. If you want to see miracles, if you want to live adventure, live generously. Give generously. Give of your time, your treasure, your talent. And never stop.

Seeds of generosity give birth to possibility. Because of Jacque's generosity, the state appointed her to a task force looking into the issue of how best to serve those who are aging out of the system. What an opportunity. What an adventure!

The adventure didn't end there. Her heart for children has now led her to Greece, where she leads teams of teachers into refugee camps, teaching and assisting the most vulnerable in the middle of the worldwide tragedy of Covid-19. This is the pioneering work, the adventure, that generosity can bring to those willing to embrace the Acts life and put our faith into action. Where will your generosity take you? What will intentionally investing in your community, your family, your church create in your own life? When we live by the Spirit (Galatians 5:25), unafraid, we can live a generous life full of possibility.

We are friends with a group of church planters in Europe called SOS. Their tagline is "We are God's Adventurers."[33] They intentionally seek to live the Acts life in every way. And you have never met a more generous group of people. Giving generously is just part of their culture. It is a habit they have cultivated. Many of them open their homes to convicted criminals exiting the prison system. Others foster children. Some spend time mentoring refugees or assisting them in finding jobs. And almost all save all year long to go to Africa on missionary trips where thousands hear the gospel and are offered free medical care and many of life's necessities. What is most astounding about this group is that the majority of their churches run without a single full-time salaried worker. They are living generously, pastoring, teaching, loving, giving without excuse. And they have found that a generous life is a life full of adventure.

Giving generously has to become a habit, not an event. When we choose to be grateful, intentional, future focused, then we find a life of adventure.

PRACTICAL TIPS FOR GENEROUS GIVING

So, where do you start? When it comes to your finances (as well as your time and expertise, for that matter), here is an easy and practical check-the-box progression for generous giving.

1) **Plan to give.**

Don't just be an emotional giver! Plan to give generously. When we plan to give, we ensure that we aren't just *feeling* generous, but we are actually acting generously. A plan to give also requires a plan for your finances as a whole. Budgeting[34] is a vital practice for personal stewardship. So, plan your finances and plan to give.

2) **Plan to give first.**

In the Old Testament (Hebrew Scriptures), there was a concept of "first fruits." Those who followed the one true God would bring the first of their harvest and their livestock to the temple. (Nehemiah 10:35-37) They would sacrifice the first to God. In the New Testament, this emphasis on the first continues. Don't just give God out of the overflow. Put your giving into your budget first rather than last.

3) **Plan to give first a portion.**

Sometimes we can be so caught up with what we don't have that we overlook what we do have. The Bible is clear that giving should be proportionate to income (Leviticus 27:30-34). In other words, we should give out of what we have, not what we don't have. Percentage giving is a great way to dedicate a portion of your income to God. Then, when your income increases, you automatically increase your portion. It is also a constant reminder that God looks at our gifts individually and our heart, most importantly, not in comparison to others.

4) **Plan to give first a portion with a cheerful heart.**

The apostle Paul, in describing how to give, said, "You must each decide in your heart how much to give. And don't give reluctantly or in response to pressure. For God loves a person who gives cheerfully." Cheerful giving comes from having a heart that is focused on God. When we focus on Him and the reality of eternity, we have a different perspective on what is in our hand to give. And what we choose to give, we can then give cheerfully. After all, at the end of life, it all goes back in the box, and we only take with us the impact we've made in people's lives and the legacy we've created with the gifts God gave us to use while on this earth.

GENEROSITY IS SO MUCH MORE THAN JUST A TITLE OR IDENTITY WE ASPIRE TO; IT IS A WHOLE WAY OF LIFE.

Generosity is so much more than just a title or identity we aspire to; it is a whole way of life. And it is crucial to living the abundant life. In the middle of the Sermon on the Mount, the keynote address from Jesus in Matthew's gospel, Jesus makes this statement: "No one can serve two masters. Either you will hate the one and love the other, or you will be devoted to the one and despise the other. You cannot serve both God and money." What Jesus is communicating is the heart of generosity and every other issue when it comes to following Him; will we follow the unseen God or put our hope in only what we can see?

Money in those verses is referring to materialism. Now, I'm not talking about needing to wear camel-hair shirts and never buy anything new. I'm not saying that having things is bad, and I don't think that is Jesus' point either. Remember, money isn't the issue, serving money is. Materialism is a way of defining your identity and your value from what you have. The Jesus way defines your identity by whose you are—God's. When we serve God, we are choosing His way over our own material identity. We are shouting "there is more!" to the world around us.

Before this verse, Jesus describes His new way of living, with a higher standard for every single issue, from love to murder to prayer. After this verse, he explains the consequences of serving money versus serving God. And the sermon ends with an exhortation to build our life on the rock of God's ways instead of the shifting sands of this world. Serving our greed, allowing it to direct our thoughts, behavior, prayers, will not lead to the stability that we crave. Only by choosing God's ways over our own can we have a life that is not shaken even by the most extreme of circumstances.

When we give generously, we reject this world's materialism and reinforce our identity as Jesus-followers. We are reminding ourselves of our focus on eternity, our role as stewards, and our commitment to obey the way of God, even in our finances. In sum, giving (planning to give first a portion) is Discipleship 101 and can lead to generosity in every other area of life if we adopt not just the habit but the heart.

Say It Again:

- Generosity started with God—God so loved the world that he GAVE!
- Generous people are grateful.
- Generous people are intentional.
- Generous people live lives full of adventure!
- Generosity is not an event. It is a habit.
- The habit of giving looks like planning to give first a portion with a cheerful heart.
- The heart of giving is choosing to serve God over materialism.

Make it Personal:

- What simple step could you take today to make giving generously a habit in your life?
- If someone looked at your schedule or finances, would they know that you value planning to give first a portion?
- Is the habit of giving or the heart of giving a bigger challenge for you?

WE CHEER ENTHUSIASTICALLY

Nothing great was ever achieved without enthusiasm.
—RALPH WALDO EMERSON

Have you ever been in an environment where you could not help but get caught up in the excitement? I can remember my first time in Death Valley in Baton Rouge, Louisiana, watching the LSU football team take the field at Tiger Stadium. The moment the band plays, the moment the mascot roars, the moment the entire stadium stands to its feet is unlike anything I had ever experienced before. It is infectious, exciting, inspiring. You feel you are a part of something bigger than yourself, greater than the moment. And you almost cannot help but join in. There is something in us that responds to that kind of moment.

Have you ever been around a person who is so enthusiastic about life that you can't help but be a little more excited, a little more optimistic, a little more ready for what comes next? Maybe you leave their presence more convinced that your own life mission is possible and that maybe the best really is yet to come.

We all have likely known moments and people like that. And while the roar of the crowd fades, the emotion of the moment lingers. If we want to have an infectious culture, a culture that has the energy to unite, a culture that has the power to overcome obstacles, I believe we must create a culture that cheers enthusiastically.

BE CHEERFUL

> WE ARE EACH RESPONSIBLE FOR
> THE CHEER IN OUR HEARTS.

Before we talk about cheering for something, let's examine whether we are personally full of cheer. One definition of cheer is optimism or confidence. We are each responsible for the cheer in our hearts. We don't have to wait for others to cheer us up. We can cultivate a culture (attitude/philosophy/posture/mindset) of cheer within us.

It is easy to be a miserable person. Simply turn on the 24-hour news channel, tune in to talk radio, watch all the stressful dramas, listen to office gossip. There is always something in your life worth being upset over. There is most certainly always something going on in the world to take your joy.

People seem to take great pride in doing the opposite of cheering. We have internet trolls who take time, lots of time, to harass and criticize others who may have absolutely no connection to them. This may seem absurd to most of us. Who would do that? Yet, we can find ourselves creating and encouraging a culture that tears down through our words and attitudes. Sitting around scoffing at those trying to make a difference is easier than standing in the arena and trying to change culture yourself.

As a little girl, Destiny's mom taught her this scripture: "Blessed is the one who does not walk in step with the wicked or stand in the way that sinners take or sit in the company of mockers[.]" (Psalm 1:1 NIV). Blessed can also be translated as happy. If we want to be a person full of cheer, then we can't spend our days mocking others. We have to intentionally cultivate the culture of cheer inside of us.

IF YOU WANT TO BE A CHEERFUL PERSON, EXAMINE THE ENVIRONMENT YOU ARE CREATING AROUND YOU.

If you want to be a cheerful person, examine the environment you are creating around you. What do you listen to, watch, and read in your alone time? Who do you spend your time with? You don't have to stop being informed to create an environment of cheer. There are always things, people, and events around you that are worthy of notice and celebration.

This isn't a state of denial but a choice of how we want to live our lives. We don't ignore reality; after all, we are practicing honesty. Rather, we are choosing to acknowledge the bad in life and accentuate the good in our lives through our responses. When good happens, we don't sweep it under the rug; we cheer enthusiastically!

WE CAN BE OF GOOD CHEER IN ANY CIRCUMSTANCE BECAUSE OF WHO WE SERVE AND WHAT HE HAS OVERCOME!

If you are a Christ-follower, allow God's words to determine the level of your cheer. Jesus said, "These things I have spoken to you, that in Me you may have peace. In the world you will have tribulation; but be of good cheer, I have overcome the world" (John 16:33 NKJV). We can be of good cheer in any circumstance because of who we serve and what He has overcome! That should give us an optimistic mindset; the best is yet to come. And it should also give us confidence knowing God is with us.

The apostle Paul wrote to the early church, a church under the threat of persecution and dealing with all manner of difficulty, a surprising command. "Rejoice in the Lord always. I will say it again: Rejoice!" (Philippians 4:4 NIV). This seems insensitive. Yet, Paul understood that having cheer in our hearts (optimism and confidence) gives us courage for the inevitable difficulties we will face in life. Christ-followers should live a life full of cheer.

CHEER FOR YOURSELF

LEARNING TO CHEER FOR YOURSELF HELPS YOU TO RECOGNIZE THE WINS, THE PROGRESS, THE GOOD THINGS IN YOUR OWN LIFE, WHETHER OR NOT ANYONE ELSE DOES.

I once heard it said, as only a southerner could say it, "It's a sad dog that doesn't wag its own tail." I understand that we aren't to boast about ourselves and make life about our successes, but we should learn to cheer for ourselves in a healthy way. If you only see what is wrong with you, you have a distorted view of reality. That view will keep you from bringing your gifting, your generosity, your ideas to the table. And your community, organization, and even family will suffer. Learning to cheer for yourself helps you to recognize the wins, the progress, the good things in your own life, whether or not anyone else does.

Our oldest daughter has no problem cheering for herself. If you point out something she didn't do right, she will take the criticism and then remark, "But I did this part well, right?" What is she doing? She's using cheer to motivate change. If she's just losing, why should she play? But if she has part of it right, it motivates her to improve the rest.

One of the things I teach my corporate coaching clients is to celebrate improvement, not just perfection. If you are trying to start the habit of exercising, and you go three days a week when you wanted to go four, but you used to go zero, don't just note the failure of the goal. Cheer the improvement! Sure, you didn't meet your standard yet, but you were 75% of the way there. That deserves some celebration. And when you meet your goal, don't just pass it over in the name of being humble—celebrate!

///

CHEERING, CELEBRATING, RECOGNIZING WHAT GOD HAS DONE THROUGH YOU ISN'T PRIDEFUL.

\\\

An amazing woman in our church just was recognized for being in the top ten in the sales team of a national company. Top ten! That is a big deal. Yet there were people in her life who encouraged her not to celebrate in the name of humility. Cheering, celebrating, recognizing what God has done through you isn't prideful. God loves a party—just watch Jesus' life here on earth. He was always going to dinner, coming from dinner, or at dinner. Tears streamed down this amazing woman's cheeks as she told Destiny, "This church has taught me that it is okay for me to celebrate me." Cheering enthusiastically, like every other habit, starts with you! Don't wait for the world to cheer for you; choose to recognize what God is doing in your life, what has changed, what has improved, and cheer for yourself.

CHEER FOR OTHERS

///

WHEN YOU HAVE CHEER IN YOUR HEART, YOU CAN BECOME A CHEERLEADER FOR EVERYONE IN YOUR LIFE.

\\\

It is the cheer in our own hearts that makes it easier to cheer for others. When you have cheer in your heart, you can become a cheerleader for everyone in your life. Don't wait for others to cheer and then join in. Allow the cheer in your own heart to overflow into your everyday life. Another way to say this is that you have to build the attitude of cheer in your heart so that you can establish the action of cheer in your life (Proverbs 15:30; Proverbs 12:25).

A cheer is also defined as a shout of encouragement, approval, or congratulations.[35] It is an intentional and vocal act. It requires energy and focus. Think of your favorite sports team. In an arena near you, some people are putting forth some serious effort to cheer. They aren't cheering politely. They are cheering enthusiastically!

In our home, you will find us cheering for every victory. In fact, if we fail to cheer, even the smallest child in the family will remind us. When Carolina, our oldest, was only two or three, she did something cute and didn't get the appropriate response. She grabbed Destiny's cheeks and said, "Momma, clap for me!" We cheer enthusiastically! This habit goes beyond cheering for our team or our family. When we say that we have a habit of cheering enthusiastically, we mean that we have already pre-decided our response to the success of others.

Here is what happens when you cheer for others:

1) **You give energy.** This is a main reason why we often don't cheer. It takes energy, and exerting energy takes practice! When we cheer, we are giving energy to others. We give that energy through our words, our expressions, our body language, and even our text emojis.

2) **They feel enthusiasm.** We will get to the meaning of enthusiasm later in this chapter, but for now, remember that your energy has an impact on the feelings of others. Think about how it feels when someone cheers for you! There is a transfer of energy and excitement. It is a validation of your hard work and accomplishment (or just your existence!).

3) **They take in encouragement.** This world tries to rob courage from everyone. When we cheer enthusiastically, it isn't just a momentary transfer of energy. No. We leave people with more courage for the next mission, the next obstacle, the next challenge.

CHEERING FOR OTHERS TAKES NOTHING AWAY FROM YOU

Destiny's dad was a football coach, specifically an offensive coordinator. He taught her a lot about offense. When they would watch games, they would cheer for offense. Not a team. Just the offense, whoever had the ball. They celebrated every score regardless of the team. The truth is, in life, I want to cheer for you! I don't want to pick a side. I want everyone to score. This is a silly example, and I hope, think, believe most of us have a favorite sports team that we love to cheer for in whatever sport we play. However, it is a good illustration of the choices we get to make when we choose to cheer enthusiastically. We don't have to choose sides. We can cheer for everyone.

This is something we are actively teaching our children. Not long ago, one of our daughters received a very generous gift. Her grandparents bought her a new guitar. It is beautiful. On the way back from the store, her older sister was having a hard time cheering for her. Her sister was primarily occupied with "How is this going to affect me?" "When do I get my big gift?" "Does this mean I'm not as important?" Those may seem like a child's questions, but every time someone is promoted at work or gets a better grade at school or is able to take the vacation we wanted for ourselves, those questions pop up like lost socks, always there when you don't need them.

CHEERING FOR OTHERS COMES FROM BEING FULL OF OPTIMISM AND CONFIDENCE.

The truth is there is room for all of us. Cheering for others comes from being full of optimism and confidence. When those things are lacking, it feels like every cheer for someone else takes away something from us. My youngest daughter developed a habit of asking every time someone else in the family was complimented, "Are you proud of me too?" She is asking, "Is there room for me too?" And the answer to her and to you is, "YES!" There is room. A mindset of scarcity will lead to a life of stingy behavior and a lot less cheering. One of the saddest moments of the musical *Hamilton* is when Aaron Burr (who shoots Hamilton in a duel) says there was enough room in the world for Hamilton and me. He realized it too late. You don't have to do the same. You can cultivate cheer in your heart and then cheer for others without taking anything away from you. There is room!

> IF I'M ALWAYS CHEERING FOR THE KINGDOM
> OF GOD, THERE IS ALWAYS SOMEONE
> OR SOMETHING TO CHEER FOR!

One of our great joys is cheering for other churches, other ministries, other businesses, other pastors in our area. As Christ-followers, we are part of a global church. And in the grand scheme of things, our church, any church, is just a small expression of God's kingdom on the earth. If I'm only cheering for me and mine, I miss out on many opportunities to cheer. Even when things aren't going so well for "us," there is someone somewhere doing great things and making a massive impact on their community, and my habit turns their success into my own. One of the keys to cheering is to choose a bigger "us" to cheer for. If I'm always cheering for the kingdom of God, there is always someone or something to cheer for!

CHEER EVEN WHEN OTHERS JEER

> OUR GOAL IS NOT TO PARTICIPATE IN CULTURE
> BUT TO CHALLENGE AND CHANGE CULTURE.

Cheering for others is counter-cultural. We compete with others. We cheer for our team, our family, our guy. The world struggles with cheering, but it is great at jeering. The pattern of the world is criticism, ridicule, heckling, scoffing, and taunting. Our goal is not to participate in culture but to challenge and change culture. We cheer in the face of their jeer.

A well-known preacher was written about online very cruelly by a blogger who had never even met her. Instead of responding in anger, she wrote the blogger a nice note, ending it with "I'm cheering for you." She chose to cheer in the face of the jeer. Why? Because she has decided that regardless of what others say or do, she will cheer, encourage, build up, and be a fan. She has decided not to choose sides but to cheer for everyone.

CHEERING SENDS A MESSAGE

What I love about cheering for others is the message that it sends. Destiny taught me to think this way. I tend to encourage myself and assume everyone else does the same. I have learned that my cheer sends a message that is needed and appreciated by those around me. This is the message:

1) **I see you**. In a world where people often feel isolated and invisible, cheering shows them that they are seen and appreciated.

2) **I believe in you**. When I take the time to cheer, I'm not just speaking to someone's present, but also their future. We are speaking that their future is worth investing energy into. We are showing in a practical way that we believe in them!

3) **I want you to win**. When I cheer, I let those around me know that they don't have to hide their greatness or gifting. They don't have to whisper about their accomplishment to keep me from feeling intimidated. Instead, they know without a doubt that I want them to win and keep winning.

As a Christ-follower, cheering is part of me delivering the message of hope that I find in the gospel. God sees us, believes in us, wants us to win. And when I cheer those around me, I am sending the same message and opening their hearts to the bigger truth of His love and His purpose for their life.

CHEERING FOR OTHERS MAKES A DIFFERENCE

*There is a real magic in enthusiasm. It spells the difference
between mediocrity and accomplishment.*
—NORMAN VINCENT PEALE

Destiny's grandfather loved God and loved people. He was known for many things; he was a local church pastor for over forty years. What he may be best known for was the way that he cheered for those around him. He called everyone he encountered "Champion." And when he died, person after person cried telling the family how his cheer changed their life. His words changed the way they saw themselves.

In Death Valley, the crowd knows they have a part to play. They can't replace good coaching or hard work in the off season, but they can add something extra—an extra dose of courage that may just make the difference for the boys of fall. We can't put in the work for those around us. We can't make good choices for them or create a great internal culture for them. We CAN choose to cheer for them and instill some courage into their hearts. And it might just make the difference.

> IT COSTS SO LITTLE, BUT YOUR CHEER CAN
> CREATE A LIFEGIVING CULTURE, EVEN IF IT'S
> JUST FOR A MOMENT, FOR OTHERS.

Cheering certainly makes a difference in the culture around you. I love to walk into a coffee shop or quick-service restaurant and greet everyone with cheer and enthusiasm. Answering "How are you?" with "I'm wonderful—and excited to be here!" is a surprise to most in the service industry every time. These essential workers often bear the brunt of poor behavior. Cheering for them, thanking them, bringing energy to their environment can literally change the mood of the day and even the entire room. It costs so little, but your cheer can create a lifegiving culture, even if it's just for a moment, for others.

YOU HAVE THE POWER THROUGH YOUR CHEER TO COMFORT AND SUPPORT.

Cheer is also defined as giving comfort or support to someone. People around you need comfort and support. They are encountering battles you know about and ones you have no idea about and never will. You have the power through your cheer to comfort and support. I think if you are reading this book that you likely want to be that sort of person. Unfortunately, most people who are hurting or going through a difficult time don't wear a button that says, "I really need some cheer today." When we consistently cheer, we are able to meet the needs of those around us even when we aren't fully aware of their circumstance.

Destiny has a true habit of cheering for others with all her heart. And what I have found is that it opens the door for perfect strangers to share their lives and their struggles with her. She will cheerfully greet someone taking our order, ask about their life, and cheer their direction, whether it is nursing school or a new pet. Suddenly, walls go down, and she often ends up praying for the less cheerful parts of their lives. You never know the difference your cheer will make, but know it will make a difference.

WE CHEER . . . ENTHUSIASTICALLY!

We want to not only cheer but cheer enthusiastically. We stand up a lot at NCC. We cheer for special guests. We cheer for baptisms. We cheer for babies being dedicated. We cheer for our kids. We cheer for servant-leaders. We cheer enthusiastically! No golf clap kinds of cheering allowed. We are looking for over-the-top, authentic, sincere, from-the-heart, loud cheering. The root of the word enthusiasm is enthous. It literally means to be possessed by a god.[36] And that is how we cheer because we are possessed by the one true God. We don't cheer mildly. We cheer wildly!

WE CHEER FROM THE CORE OF OUR BEING BECAUSE THAT IS HOW GOD CHEERS FOR US.

We cheer from the core of our being because that is how God cheers for us. Do you believe that? Is that how you see God? Or do you see Him continually frowning and disappointed with you?

Enthusiasm, cheering enthusiastically, must become a habit. It is difficult to vocally cheer for others if you aren't cheerful in your own heart. We have to *choose* to live possessed, to live an inspired life. The apostle Paul admonished the early church in Rome. "Never be lazy, but work hard and serve the Lord enthusiastically" (Romans 12:11 NLT). Never be lazy. Never be without enthusiasm. That is a choice. We have to train ourselves to be enthusiastic.

Enthusiasm comes from our inner dialogue. When our inner dialogue is not right, it is nearly impossible for our external dialogue to be cheerful. If, on the other hand, I am telling myself the right things, creating enthusiasm in my life, then I am able to give that enthusiasm away! I cheer enthusiastically because I have learned to cheer internally!

APPOINT YOURSELF CHEERLEADER FOR EVERYONE IN YOUR LIFE AND CHEER THEM ENTHUSIASTICALLY!

Choose to cheer! Don't wait for someone else to start the standing ovation. Don't wait for someone else to applaud. Don't wait for someone else to approve. Appoint yourself cheerleader for everyone in your life and cheer them enthusiastically! It will make all the difference in your home, your business, your church, and your community.

Say it Again:

- We can be cheerful!
- Cheering for others comes from being personally full of cheer.
- You are responsible for your internal cheer.
- Cultivating your environment and inner dialogue will help you stay full of cheer even in difficult circumstances.
- Cheer gives us courage!
- We can cheer for others!
- Cheering is a pre-decided response to the success and even presence of others.
- Cheering does not take anything away from you. There is room.
- You can cheer even when others jeer.
- Cheering for others makes a difference.
- We can cheer enthusiastically!
- Enthusiasm comes from a word that means possessed by the gods.
- We should be enthusiastic as Christ-followers because we have the spirit of Christ on the inside of us.
- Enthusiasm is not about volume; it is about intention.
- Enthusiasm comes from our inner dialogue and can be cultivated regardless of our personality.
- You don't have to wait for anyone else's approval or action to begin cheering enthusiastically; you can be the cheerleader!

Make it Personal:

- How do you see God? Is He angry with you or cheering for you?
- Are you cheerful? What inputs might you eliminate or add to your life to change your internal and external dialogue?
- Who can you cheer for today?
- Is it hard for you to cheer for the success of others? Allow God to show you that the success of others does not reduce your own value to Him.
- Make a choice to cultivate an enthusiastic cheer. Practice at work, at church, in your home.

WE STAY ON MISSION

There is always a way - if you're committed
—Tony Robbins

///

IT'S EASY TO LET LIFE DIVERT YOU FROM YOUR MISSION.

\\

Have you ever walked into a room and realized you have completely forgotten why you are there to begin with? It's easy to let life divert you from your mission, whatever it is. This habit is the exclamation point for all the rest. No matter what happens, we have already pre-decided to stay on mission. Make no mistake, staying on mission will need to be habitual. Coach Vince Lombardi said, "Most people fail, not because of lack of desire, but because of lack of commitment." We may desire to achieve the mission, but ultimately, it will be our commitment to stay on mission, get back on mission, and keep going in the face of apathy or adversity or even forgetfulness that will make the difference.

YOU MUST HAVE A MISSION TO STAY ON MISSION

*Commitment is doing the thing you said you were going to
do long after the mood you said it in has left you.*
—Darren Hardy

Remember that mission from the beginning of the book? Jesus gave us a mission. "Therefore, go and make disciples of all the nations, baptizing them in the name of the Father and the Son and the Holy Spirit. Teach these new disciples to obey all the commands I have given you" (Matthew 28:19–20 NLT). We just reworded it for our context—creating Christ-centered, culture-changing community.

///

OUR HABITS CAN BECOME ABOUT US IF WE DON'T KEEP THE MISSION FRONT AND CENTER.

\\

Before you can "Stay on Mission," you must realize that you have a mission. Our habits can become about us if we don't keep the mission front and center. Yes, cheering enthusiastically, loving big, giving generously, practicing honesty will make your life better. Yes, growing intentionally, leaning in, and leading out will expand your capacity. Yes, living on, protecting unity, and embracing discipline will improve your relationships. That is not the point. There is more. There is much more.

We have a mission. And we have to stay focused on that mission. Staying on mission must become more than a mantra. It has to be a habit. It has to become a ready response to those things that would distract us and keep us from God's best. It has to become the encouraging word to redirect our focus from what is trivial to what is eternal.

Jesus is not the positivity preacher that many portray Him as today. He was extremely honest—sometimes brutally so. John, chapter sixteen, starts with some very stark declarations. "They will put you out of the synagogue; in fact, the time is coming when anyone who kills you will think they are offering a service to God." That's not encouraging Jesus. Yet, He is preparing His followers for the reality of their mission. Following Jesus would cost them everything. And in giving their lives for the mission, they would literally change the course of human history and, ultimately, the world. He ends the chapter not by softening his prophecy, but by offering Himself. "I have told you these things, so that in me you may have peace. In this world you will have trouble. But take heart! I have overcome the world."

There are plenty of things that will try to knock you off your mission. Whether they come from the nature of the mission or from just living in this world, remember that nothing you face is unique to you! We all face the same types of obstacles. And if someone else has overcome what you currently face, you can too.

DISCOURAGEMENT

> *Develop success from failures. Discouragement and failure*
> *are two of the surest stepping stones to success.*
> —DALE CARNEGIE

WHEN WE FAIL, WE HAVE THE CHOICE TO WALLOW IN DISCOURAGEMENT OR TO LEARN AND KEEP GOING.

Discouragement will try to separate you from your mission. Discouragement is probably most accurately described as a loss of courage—literally being separated from courage. When we fail, we have the choice to wallow in discouragement or to learn and keep going. John Maxwell wrote a book called *Sometimes You Win; Sometimes You Learn*. The entire book could have been that one phrase and it would have been enough. Discouragement takes your courage; learning reminds you that you can keep going and take the lessons from today into tomorrow.

Is there an area of your life where you lack courage today? Are you stuck in a cycle of discouragement that started with a failure but has resulted in a stalled mission? I encourage you to take time, write down your fears, your feelings, your failures. Then, turn the page and write what you have learned. Think about how you can use this failure or discouragement as a stepping stone forward. If we want to stay on mission, we have to face discouragement and let it fuel us rather than stall us.

DISCOURAGEMENT BLINDS YOU TO WHAT
GOD DID IN THE PAST AND WHAT GOD IS
CAPABLE OF DOING IN YOUR FUTURE!

As a Christ-follower, we can look to the Word of God for courage. Approximately 360 times in the Bible, God says, "Do not fear." Why? Because if you want to stay on mission, it will require courage. Discouragement blinds you to what God did in the past and what God is capable of doing in your future! When you move apart from courage, panic sets in. In moments of discouragement, we have to choose to be calm and to remember who we serve and what He has overcome.

DISTRACTION

Don't dwell on what went wrong. Instead, focus on what to do next. Spend your energies on moving forward toward finding the answer.
—Denis Waitley

Distraction will try to knock you off mission. One of my favorite things to do is laugh, and people or circumstances who make me laugh are my favorite. I am of the slap-stick comedy generation. So I have at times found myself laughing for much longer than necessary at videos of people falling or tripping. Have you seen the videos of people on their phones walking straight into a pond outdoors or a water fountain in the mall? We laugh, but we also know the feeling of complete distraction that blinds us from everything around us. Maybe you were driving and arrived at your destination without really remembering the drive. Maybe you finished dinner with your spouse or friend and realized you hadn't really heard a thing that was said. Distraction takes moments. And if we aren't careful, it will knock us off more than our feet; it will knock us off mission.

DISTRACTIONS CAN COME ON THE MOUNTAINTOP AFTER YOUR GREATEST VICTORY OR DOWN IN THE VALLEY AFTER YOUR WORST DEFEAT.

Distractions can even be good things that keep me from pursuing my ultimate mission, things like career or relationships or significance. Distractions can come on the mountaintop after your greatest victory or down in the valley after your worst defeat. Regardless of when distraction comes, it is our habit of staying on mission that keeps us on the right path. We see ourselves or our families beginning to veer, and we readjust our course. Don't allow distraction to win. Stay on mission.

There are the basic distractions and business of life: groceries, kids, social dinners, bills. There are the fun distractions: phones, social media, movies, shows, video games. There are emotional distractions: last night's argument, today's big meeting, next week's doctor's appointment. So many distractions surround us. It can feel like a flurry of activity. How can anyone respond to the reality around them, much less live with intention on mission?

Let me encourage you. Missional living is possible. It will take effort and practice, but it is possible. In our church community, we teach that if we want to advance in life, we must have the right stance. Yes, it rhymes. That helps us remember! We describe our stance as having two foundations: excellence and resilience. Excellence keeps driving us forward toward mission. Resilience keeps us practicing getting back up over and over again, even in the face of disappointment or discouragement, or distraction. If we don't have one, we won't advance. We need both.

Here are some practical tools that can help you to move past distraction to missional living.

1) **A calendar** – using your calendar, scheduling tasks, and then doing your best to review and stick to the schedule is a great way to avoid the stress of the last minute. It's not perfect, but it is a

must-have tool in the stay-on-mission toolkit. The Full Focus Planner by Michael Hyatt was a game changer for me. There are many goal/schedule systems; try some out and find a method that works for you.

2) **Meditation[37] or quiet time** – letting your mind clear and focus is both a skill and a key to dealing with distraction. For Christ-followers, we are instructed to meditate on the words of God. This lets us clear our minds from things that are clouding the way toward our mission. Even five minutes a day can be a game changer. I truly believe five minutes of meditation before the day will do more for you than five extra minutes of sleep ever will.

IF YOU WANT TO SAY YES TO MISSION, YOU WILL HAVE TO SAY NO TO SOMETHING.

3) **Limits** – If you want to say YES to mission, you will have to say NO to something. Social media and mindless screen-watching are easy time wasters. Remember, it's about starting with your YES and then letting NO come from those choices. If your calendar is full of mission, you will not have time for as much distraction. My motto here: I have a choice!

Distraction isn't just about eliminating the frivolous or improved planning. It can also be about winning the game in our minds. Distraction in our thoughts often increases with distance or difficulty. "I thought I was going to arrive there faster. I thought this was going to happen quicker. I expected this to be easier." Our inner dialogue of doubt can begin to focus us on what has not been accomplished rather than the mission we serve. When we realize how far we still have to go, we can get distracted. We can lose focus on the mission and get caught up in the mundane.

WE CAN CHOOSE TO TRUST THAT GOD WILL WORK WHAT IS OUTSIDE OF OUR CONTROL, ULTIMATELY, FOR GOOD.

Proverbs warns us, "Keep vigilant watch over your heart; that's where life starts. Don't talk out of both sides of your mouth; avoid careless banter, white lies, and gossip. Keep your eyes straight ahead; ignore all sideshow distractions. Watch your step, and the road will stretch out smooth before you. Look neither right nor left; leave evil in the dust" (Proverbs 4:23–27 MSG). Look neither right nor left. Our eyes in scripture often are representative of our focus. When fighting the battle of our mind, we must focus on what we can control, not what we cannot. We can control the way we love others today. We can control our attitude. We can choose to get better today and lean in more closely. And as Christians, we can choose to trust that God will work what is outside of our control, ultimately, for good.

DISASTER

When trouble comes, focus on God's ability to care for you.
—Charles Stanley

Sometimes the unexpected happens. Sometimes it devastates us. In Louisiana, we are accustomed to hurricanes. In the north, more years than not, we hear about a storm, lose power, or deal with a bit of flooding. Life quickly gets back to normal. In the south, it is a much different situation. Hurricanes bring disasters that linger in communities for years, even decades. They upend lives and force difficult questions like, "Do we stay? Do we try to rebuild again? Why do we have to keep starting over?" One of our denomination's leaders explained it this way. It is one thing to go and serve a devastated community. It is another thing to serve a devastated community and then go home to your own devastated home or FEMA trailer.

Maybe your life feels like a hurricane has hit—debris everywhere, uncomfortable questions, and a feeling of helpless hopelessness. You keep showing up for others, but you are going back home to your own private disaster. I want you to know I am so sorry. We grieve with you. And you must grieve well. Find a counselor who can help walk you through. Be patient with yourself and those around you who don't quite get it or know what to say.

A SENSE OF MISSION–A BELIEF THAT ONE'S LIFE MATTERS–PROVIDES A WHY THAT CAN CARRY US THROUGH.

Staying on mission doesn't mean life never hands you disaster. It also doesn't mean we ignore or lie about what we are facing. The amazing thing about staying on mission is that this habit can give you strength and meaning in the midst of even the worst disaster. Viktor Frankl, Holocaust survivor, psychologist, and author, wrote, "Those who have a 'why' to live, can bear with almost any 'how'." A sense of mission—a belief that one's life matters—provides a why that can carry us through.

Being knocked permanently off mission by disaster isn't inevitable. You can still stay on mission. And that mission will help you to walk through your own personal disaster. It has been said life doesn't wait on the wounded. That is most certainly true. However, it is also true that heroism isn't reserved for those in the best of times, but most often the providence of those who choose to stay on mission in the worst of times. In other words, your wound, your disaster, your pain does not disqualify you. Only our own response can truly move us off mission.

Here are three responses to disaster that can help you stay on mission:

1) **Choose gratitude**. When disaster hits, it is easy to allow the pain of the moment to become our only focus. Gratitude allows us to acknowledge the negative but focus on the positive or the

possibilities. Try starting each morning with writing three things you are grateful for and making it a different three each day.

YOU CAN CHOOSE TO IDENTIFY AS A VICTIM OR A SURVIVOR, AND THAT ONE CHOICE CAN MAKE A WORLD OF DIFFERENCE.

2) **Choose your story**. I'm not talking about choosing your facts. If a hurricane destroys your house, it is ludicrous to pretend it was a planned demolition. However, you have a choice whether to live in a story where all your hopes and dreams are destroyed or where you are in the midst of rebuilding. You can choose to identify as a victim or a survivor, and that one choice can make a world of difference. Try speaking out loud your current story— can you change your identity or narrative to take back the power and allow yourself to move forward?

3) **Choose to focus on what you can control**. You can't control the weather. You can't control the insurance company. You can't even control the prejudices or pain or choices of others. You can control your response, your path, and your next right thing. I encourage you to be resolute about focusing on what you can control. Maybe it is as simple as controlling the music you listen to while you clean up the debris. Maybe it is choosing to speak encouraging words or do something intentional for someone else around you. There is something in your environment that you can control. So identify it, take control of it, and refuse to focus on the things outside your control.

In any environment, we aren't just responding to the things in life that knock us off mission, but we should also be intentionally cultivating those things that will keep us on mission. To say it a different way, pulling weeds is only one part of growing a garden. You also need to plant seeds. Here are a few seeds that should be a part of every life that wishes to stay on mission.

DREAMS KEEP YOU ON MISSION

FOR CHRIST-FOLLOWERS, DREAMING ABOUT HEAVEN ISN'T A DISTRACTION; IT'S AN INSPIRATION.

Dreams are visualizations of the life we are trying to build, the difference we are hoping to make. For Christ-followers, dreaming about heaven isn't a distraction; it's an inspiration. Imagining what it will be like when your family is all in church serving God isn't fantasy; it is a necessity. Planning generosity as you build your business isn't peripheral; it is central. Don't lose sight of your dream. The dream will motivate you when nobody else will.

The dream will focus you when nobody else can.

THE LONG-TERM DREAM KEEPS THE SHORT-TERM STRUGGLES IN PERSPECTIVE.

What is it that you are trying to accomplish? This is why we remind ourselves every single week as a congregation that we are on a mission to create Christ-centered, culture-changing community in our homes, businesses, and city. This is why we place kids and babies and teens at the core of our programs because we want to leave a legacy for the next generation. The long-term dream keeps the short-term struggles in perspective. If all you see is the struggle, you will struggle to stay on mission.

DETERMINATION KEEPS YOU ON MISSION

When we keep the dream in front of us, we activate determination within us. Isaiah described God-given determination this way: "Because the Sovereign Lord helps me, I will not be disgraced. Therefore, I have set my face like a stone, determined to do his will. And I know that I will not be put to shame" (Isaiah 50:7 NLT). In other words, I am determined not to be deterred.

> GRIT IS THAT RELENTLESS DETERMINATION THAT REFUSES TO GIVE IN, GIVE OUT, OR GIVE UP.

Another word for determination is grit. In athletics, the most talented team doesn't always win the game. Sometimes they get out-hustled, and experience has shown that hustle will typically beat talent if talent doesn't hustle. Grit doesn't care about the odds or predictions, nor does it care about what people think should happen. Grit also isn't overwhelmed by the challenges in front of it or the adversity around it. Grit will find a way to win. Grit is that relentless determination that refuses to give in, give out, or give up. Grit doesn't stop when it's losing. Grit doesn't hang its head when things are not going well. Instead, grit keeps fighting, keeps believing, and stays on mission.

> DETERMINATION IS THE SOMETHING EXTRA THAT ALLOWS US TO STAY ON MISSION IN THE MIDST OF THE STORM, WHEN OTHERS QUIT, AND IT WOULD BE EASIER TO WALK AWAY.

One custom that has helped us stay on mission with determination is breaking the dream into dashes. You can't see the finish line of a marathon, but you can easily see the finish line of the 100-yard dash. As a church, we break our dream down into quarterly, yearly, and five-year dashes. As a family, we create short-term goals and immediate tangible objectives that must be accomplished along the journey. The dashes help us stay focused because we can see and feel the progress we are making. If you are feeling stuck, overwhelmed, underprepared, it is time to create a dash and check something off the list. God's dream is too big for your life or your lifetime. So, create winnable moments and celebrate the dashes on the way to the dream.

ATTENTION WILL KEEP US ON MISSION

Proverbs advises us, "Look straight ahead, and fix your eyes on what lies before you. Mark out a straight path for your feet; stay on the safe path" (Proverbs 4:25–25 NLT). This is actually really good driving advice. I've seen people not only talk and text while driving but do makeup and hair, eat salads, and educate their children. (Destiny is looking very guilty at this moment.) Solomon isn't writing driving advice. He is writing life advice. "Look straight ahead, and fix your eyes on what lies before you."

WHATEVER HAS YOUR ATTENTION HAS YOU.

In life, you feel tension for your attention. There are so many things that are fighting for our attention. In fact, there are entire industries (marketing!) that exist to divert your attention for profit. Whatever has your attention has you. It has your time, your energy, your thoughts, and ultimately even your money. Examine what has your attention today. What are you focusing on when it comes to your thoughts, your schedule, your energy?

Staying on mission will require me to focus my attention on what matters most to accomplishing the mission in this season. The book you hold in your hand came from focused attention. Destiny and I have thousands of things that could distract us from writing. We have kids and a church and multiple businesses. Writing this book, and accomplishing the mission of finishing this manuscript, took focusing our attention and saying no to distractions.

How do you keep your attention focused? One way is to utilize daily declarations.

1) **Write it down**: make sure that your mission is clear, written, and that you review it regularly.

2) **Plan**: what one thing are you doing today to move the mission forward? What is next for you on your mission journey? What we plan for, we tend to focus on.

3) **Evaluate**: how is your missional living journey going? Are you staying focused 30% of the time, 10%? Don't get discouraged; make incremental growth your goal, not perfection.

4) **Cultivate accountability**: when you are living on mission in community, it is easier to stay focused. Who in your life shares your mission or can help you stay accountable to move forward?

DECISION IS REQUIRED TO STAY ON MISSION

Decision is the act of making up one's mind.[38] I like to think about decision as the seat belt that keeps me squarely in place, on mission, during the wild ride of life. It is an absolute requirement for your journey and essential to staying on mission. Sometimes we try to live on mission the way we would test drive a car. We are driving, but we aren't taking ownership. Every moment we are evaluating and reevaluating whether this car is really the one for us. Eventually, you have to stop test-driving the car and make a decision. Then, the real journey can begin!

Tony Robbins says, "It is in your moments of decision that your destiny is shaped." And living on mission requires a decision that is renewed every single day. I love the way that the late Myles Munroe said it: "Our life is the sum total of all the decisions we make every day[.]" In other words, your initial decision to stay on mission must be followed up by daily decisions to stay on mission.

One of my favorite daily decision tools is our family declaration.[39] When we leave our house, my son yells to the top of his voice, "It's declaration time!" And it begins.

God, this is your day.

I am yours.

Let's go for it.

I am brave. I am bold. I am blessed.

I am strong. I am fast. I am built to last.

I listen well. I work hard. I never give up.

Holy Spirit, open up my eyes to see, my ears to hear, my mind

to understand everything that God has for me today.

In Jesus' name, Amen!

What is that all about? I am teaching them to make a daily declaration of their decision to live life on mission. What is your declaration? Have you decided to live life on mission?

For Christ-followers, living on mission begins with "I have decided to follow Jesus."

If you've never had that moment, I want to invite you to make your decision. Jesus loves you, and His sacrifice is for you! You can choose today to follow Jesus by simply declaring your intent to follow Him through prayer. Say this simple prayer:

"Jesus, I believe you are God. I believe you died for me so I could live the abundant life and have eternal life. I want to follow you. Teach me how to do that every single day."

Yes, missional living is a journey, but it is also a decision. As the proverb says, "The journey of a thousand miles begins with one step." What have you decided?

Have you decided to live on? Love big? Lean in? Lead out? Have you decided that your mission is worth your life? Until you make the decision, you are simply test-driving life. An intentional life, a life of mission, requires a decision.

Say It Again:
- You must have a mission to stay on mission.
- There are things in life that will try to knock you off mission.
  - › You can stay on mission regardless of your circumstances.
  - › Discouragement, distraction, and disaster are common challenges to staying on mission.
- We can create a life that stays on mission by nurturing certain behaviors and thought patterns.
  - › When we dream, visualize our future, we help ourselves to stay focused on the mission.
  - › Determination is the something extra that allows us to stay on mission in the midst of the storm, when others quit, and it would be easier to walk away.
  - › Our attention is focused on practical daily steps.
- Living on mission starts with a decision, and staying on mission requires you to make that decision daily.

Make it Personal:
- How can you keep the mission of your life in front of you every single day?
- Are your dreams connected to your mission?
- Have you broken your dream into dashes to help you stay on mission?
- What can you do to cultivate the determination and grit necessary to stay on mission?
- Where is your attention?

CONCLUSION

ULTIMATELY, IF YOU DO NOT COMMIT TO
BUILDING INTENTIONAL HABITS, YOU ARE
COMMITTING TO YOUR LIFE STAYING THE SAME.

The culture of your house is determined by the habits of your heart and hands. Those habits will evolve intentionally or accidentally, but they will create your life. When you look at your life, what do you see? When you look at your organization, what do you see? If you don't like the culture, if you don't like the results, if you don't like the path, you can change things. And habits are one of the things that makes change possible. Ultimately, if you do not commit to building intentional habits, you are committing to your life staying the same.

If you are holding this book, I do not believe you have read this far because you want your life or organization to stay the same. There is always a price to pay for change and growth, and one of those costs is the pain and energy it takes to create habits. Twelve is not a magic number. Start with three or five or ten. If you don't know which habits you need, start with some of the ones we've presented in this book. It's not about perfection. Start with what you have and let it grow.

The habits we choose do not have to be the same habits we keep for twenty years. For us, House Habits are a living document, a blueprint of where we want to go as a community. We know that some may change or evolve over time. And your habits should change and evolve too.

Let us be clear: habits are not a magic potion for life change. They are anchors for our lives that keep the standard and mission front and center. We often fail to live up to the standard, and so will you. Stating the habits gives us a compass to guide the path of our lives—a goal to move toward. We can often be frustrated because we know we should be different, but we aren't sure exactly how or where to begin. The beauty of habits, of House Habits, is that they are written behaviors that we want to cultivate in order to achieve our mission. It's not an overnight process; it is a lifetime of daily decisions.

I challenge you to start today. Determine that your life will be mission centered and supported by intentional habits. Stop expecting the right culture to evolve in your home or organization. Instead, take control of the daily decisions and thought processes that create your culture. Use these habits, your habits, to change the trajectory of your family, your church, your school, your business, and your life. Our mission, as Christ-followers, is too important to be left to chance. Be intentional, missional, and relentless in your pursuit of seeing God's kingdom come to earth. And know that we are cheering enthusiastically for you.

ENDNOTES

Mission Focused

1 Stephen Covey, *How to Develop Your Personal Mission Statement* (Grand Haven, Michigan: Grand Harbor Press, 2013).

2 John C. Maxwell, *Developing the Leader Within You* (Nashville: Thomas Nelson, 1993).

3 Jordan Raynor, *Called to Create: A Biblical Invitation to Create, Innovate, and Risk* (Grand Rapids: Baker Books, 2017).

4 Dallas Willard notes that WWJD isn't really the question of discipleship but rather the outcome of discipleship. For a full investigation into the spiritual disciplines see Dallas Willard, *The spirit of the disciplines: understanding how God changes lives* (San Francisco: HarperSanFrancisco, 1991).

5 https://www.phrases.org.uk/meanings/there-but-for-the-grace-of-god.html

6 Carol S. Dweck, *Mindset: The New Psychology of Success* (New York: Ballantine Books, 2006). https://drleaf.com

7 https://keithcraft.org

8 https://churchonthemove.com

Habit One: We Live On

9 https://www.dictionary.com/browse/habit; https://www.dictionary.com/browse/acquire; https://www.dictionary.com/browse/behavior; https://www.merriam-webster.com/dictionary/pattern. All accessed September 2, 2022.

10 Hal Hershfield, "You Make Better Decisions If You 'See' Your Senior Self," *Harvard Business Review*, June 2013, https://hbr.org/2013/06/you-make-better-decisions-if-yo u-see-your-senior-self.

11 Lake, Brandon, Christopher Joel Brown, Steven Furtick and Tiffany Hammer. *My Testimony,* (Bethel Music, Essential Music Publishing, 2020).

12 John Adams, *The Adams-Jefferson Letters: The Complete Correspondence Between Thomas Jefferson and Abigail and John Adams.* New York: Simon & Schuster, 1971. "I could fill volumes with descriptions of temples and palaces, paintings, sculptures, tapestry, porcelain, etc., etc., etc.—if I could have time. But I could not do this without neglecting my duty. The science of government it is my duty to study, more than all other sciences: the art of legislation and administration and negotiation, ought to take place, indeed to exclude in a manner all other arts. I must study politics and war that my sons may have liberty to study mathematics and

philosophy. My sons ought to study mathematics and philosophy, geography, natural history, naval architecture, navigation, commerce, and agriculture, in order to give their children a right to study painting, poetry, music, architecture, statuary, tapestry, and porcelain."

13 Nancy Herndon, "The 28 Oaks of Oak Alley. Every Tree of This Ancient Enchanted Forest Still Stands." *The Christian Science Monitor*, December 2, 1988, https://www.csmonitor. com/1988/1202/hoak.html.

14 https://www.lexico.com/en/definition/trust

15 Brianna Steinhilber, "The Health Benefits of Working Out with a Crowd," *NBC News BETTER*, September 15, 2017, https://www.nbcnews.com/better/health/ why-you-should-work-out-crowd-ncna798936.

Habit Two: We Love Big

16 See note 6 and Juliana Breines, "3 Ways Your Beliefs Can Shape Your Reality," *Psychology Today*, August 30, 2015, https://www.psychologytoday.com/us/blog/in-love-and-war/20150 8/3-ways-your-beliefs-can-shape-your-reality.

Habit Three: We Protect Unity

17 Unity should NEVER be an excuse for abuse. If you are being abused in your home, your church, or your business, leave. Get help. Talk to a professional. Nothing in this book should be interpreted as an excuse to allow others to hurt you and your family. We protect unity does not mean protecting abusers from the lawful consequences of their choices.

Habit Four: We Honor Consistently

18 https://www.merriam-webster.com/dictionary/honorable

Habit Five: We Lean In

19 Jenna Jonaitis, "These 12 Exercises Will Help You Reap the Health Benefits of Good Posture," *Healthline*, https://www.healthline.com/health/fitness-exercise/ posture-benefits#1.; https://www.usa.edu/blog/how-to-improve-posture/.

20 https://www.livestrong.com/article/197390-posture-nonverbal-communication/

21 Brianna Steinhilber, "The Health Benefits of Working Out with a Crowd," *NBC News BETTER*, September 15, 2017, https://www.nbcnews.com/better/health/ why-you-should-work-out-crowd-ncna798936.

Habit Six: We Grow Intentionally

22 Peter Piñon is a counselor, cognitive coach, and speaker. He has had a profound influence on Destiny and me in a very short period of time. He can be found at https://mindsconnected.com.

23 Carroll Doherty, "We're Stuck at the Same Level of Ignorance," *The New York Times*, October 2, 2015, https://www.nytimes.com/roomfordebate/2012/10/22/reading-more-but-learning-less/were-stuck-at-the-same-level-of-ignorance.

24 One practice strategy is creating if-thens for the various obstacles I may face. For example, if I am growing my trust in God, I will create if-thens for fear, worry, discouragement. IF I feel afraid...I will quote this scripture. IF I worry...I will pray this prayer. IF I feel discouraged...I will make this declaration. By pre-planning my responses, I've turned every potential obstacle into an opportunity to grow.

25 Many people could be credited with saying that leaders are learners. Here is one of my favorite quotes from Pastor Rick Warren on the subject: "All leaders are learners. The moment you stop learning, you stop leading. I learn as much as I can, from as many as I can, as often as I can."

Habit Seven: We Practice Honesty

26 https://www.merriam-webster.com/dictionary/honesty

27 A big obstacle for many in practicing honesty around difficult realities like racism is the pride that says, "This isn't my fault. Why should I care." Of course, only those who do not confront racism on a daily basis, in a very personal way, can even take such a stance. Practicing honesty allows me to listen and grieve or even apologize regardless of my personal guilt. In fact, I begin to disappear in the conversation as I simply try to connect. Here is an example. A young man in our church named Ben (not his real name) was in the Air Force and a new American citizen. After one of our cultural conversations, in one of the back rooms, I simply asked him to share his own stories of encountering prejudice. He shared as tears fell down his face. In that moment, I apologized. I begged his forgiveness, not as a perpetrator, but as a peacemaker. We practiced honesty together and it connected our hearts.

Habit Eight: We Embrace Discipline

28 Carol S. Dweck, *Mindset: The New Psychology of Success* (New York: Ballantine Books, 2006).

29 Dallas Willard, *The Spirit of the Disciplines: Understanding How God Changes Lives* (San Francisco: HarperSanFrancisco, 1991).

30 Blue Williams, "What Percentage of Gym Memberships Go Unused?" *Exercise*, July 19, 2021, https://www.exercise.com/learn/unused-gym-memberships-percentage/

Habit Nine: We Lead Out

31 See, e.g. Steven Furtick, *(Un)Qualified: How God Uses Broken People to Do Big Things* (Colorado Springs: Multnomah Books, 2016).

Habit Ten: We Give Generously

32 https://www.dictionary.com/browse/generous

33 https://sosadventure.org

34 Dave Ramsey offers many resources for learning how to budget! Don't get overwhelmed. Instead, start where you are. Take one step today. https://www.ramseysolutions.com/budgeting.

Habit Eleven: We Cheer Enthusiastically

35 https://www.dictionary.com/browse/cheer

36 https://www.merriam-webster.com/dictionary/enthusiasm#note-1

Habit Twelve: We Stay on Mission

37 Meditation is not a New Age or Eastern religious phenomenon. It is biblical and very practical. There are lots of Christian meditative practices that go all the way back to the early church and Judaism. The Bible says, "Be STILL and know that I am God." This is the essential quality of meditation for a believer. Allowing a moment of stillness to refocus us on the basic reality of life.

38 https://www.merriam-webster.com/dictionary/decision

39 Declarations can also be used to combat those pesky internal distractions. Our doubts and fears will war for our attention. It is not just what you see, but how you see it. When you look at your life, do you see your problems or His promises? Are the difficulties in life distracting you from staying on mission? Try writing down what you are believing in this season about yourself and your future. Then, say it aloud every single day. Declaring what you will focus on is a great way to intentionally direct your attention and stay on mission.

ACKNOWLEDGMENTS

On a project like this, there are so many people to thank. We have been loved big, been given the gift of honesty, and have been cheered for enthusiastically by an entire community of friends, family, and colleagues. And it would be impossible to call everyone by name in these limited paragraphs.

To our children, you are the beneficiaries of the House Habits. We pray you will always stay on mission.

To our families, the Deas and Durons, you taught us so many of the principles in this book and set us on the path to discover all the rest. Thank you for always loving and supporting us.

To our amazing NCC family, there are no words to thank you enough for teaching us how to lead and love with such grace. You are the community we have always dreamed of, but more importantly, you are creating that community everywhere you go.

A special thank you to early readers Callie Opbroek and Stacie Rathbun. Your insights were so helpful! And we could not have made it this far without our incredibly brilliant and patient first editor Susan Strecker. We hope to send you many more books in the future.

The team at Four Rivers Media have been incredible. Debbie Chand, you are a dream of a project manager. And Martijn van Tilborgh, thank you for believing in us.

To Scott and Jenni Wilson, Keith and Sheila Craft, Ron and Lynette Lewis, Peter Piñon, Scott and Kara Holmes, Johannes and Maria Amritzer, Eric and Annabelle Treuil, and every mentor, teacher, and friend we've ever had, you will find your fingerprints in these pages and on our lives. Thank you does not seem like enough.

CPSIA information can be obtained
at www.ICGtesting.com
Printed in the USA
JSHW030311060223
37306JS00004B/9